MONTANA'S
TOP BANANAS

Montana's Top Bananas

— TELL TALES ON THE WAY TO SAN FRANCISCO BAY —

Ricardo L Garcia

Montana's Top Bananas
Tell Tales
On the Way to San Francisco Bay

ISBN: 153712904X
ISBN 13: 9781537129044
Library of Congress Control Number: 2016913794
CreateSpace Independent Publishing Platform
North Charleston, South Carolina

DEDICATION

In memory of my loving parents, Clara R. & Manuel A. García

CONTENTS

WARNING

The
College Committee on Rime Crimes and Mangled Meters,
Hereby warns all previous and prospective readers,
That the fifth rendition of this here poesy book,
Should in no way, shape, or form be mistook,
For the praline prattle and gushy gabble,
Of Professors and their babble.

PROLOGUE

Of professors on their annual pilgrimage,
To reap, render and receive new knowledge,
This being a primer, handbook, and guide
Of inspirations for bucking the tide.
For all instructors, trainers, and teachers,
And all proverbially perky preachers,
Who are called to the platform or podium
To tell a tale with pepper and sodium.

Off to San Francisco we were on our way
To an annual conference by the bay,
For the first few miles we sat still and calm
So long as we had beer to serve as balm.
Wasn't long we started to fidget around,
Not a good feature when you're outward bound
On a trip to a town so far away,
We could make it, if we drove night and day.
But, the hours and miles dragged by slowly,
The beer was drunk and gone, we felt lowly,
We craved synergy to kill the time
So we thought of telling stories in rime:
A yarn, a myth, a saga, a tall tale, too,
Like Canterbury pilgrims in revue.

The pious pilgrims told stories in rime,
Punching meaning into every line,
We surmised that it would only be fair
To try the same prosody and compare,
Although we admitted we couldn't be
Half like the pilgrims of antiquity.
We would meld metered verse into terse
Sentences, avoiding blank or free verse,
And make short comments on the rimes,
So long as we spoke in rimes at all times.
Straight forward tales or ballads could pertain,
With rimed stanzas and regular refrain,
Rhetorical devices would be our pick
To mince our mangled meters quick and slick.
Contemporary speakers, it seems
Are oblivious to metrical schemes,
Most are quite content to speak in prose,
An old literary joke, I suppose.
I digress, for which there is no excuse,
The stories herein are sure to amuse,
We decided some kind of prize would go
To the best tale about folks, high or low,
Or to the best crafted story or scheme
That spieled a splendid, redeeming theme.

As you can see by these rigorous rules,
The passengers in the van were no fools,
They all held higher degrees of some kind
And rejoiced in conundrums of the mind,
Eventually, they would have to regale
Upon whom it was told the best tale,
This would occur in proper place and time,
When all's narrated in rhythm and rime.

How I managed to link up with these folks
May lend itself to jocular jabs and jokes,
Even in Missoula, U of Montana,
Where the professors are top banana.
They placed an ad in the student newspaper,
Describing their annual Spring-time caper,
A trip during Spring Break, 2001,
To recharge batteries and have some fun.
Therein, I read of them in a *Kaiman* ad,
An all-expense paid trip didn't sound bad
To this graduate student who was in need
Of a free ride to where the road might lead:
Albany, Aberdeen or Albuquerque,
Shelby, Sheboygan or Sault Sainte Marie,
Baltimore, Boston, Boise or Buffalo,
Clearwater, Calgary or Calexico,
Taos, Terre Haute, Tulsa or Toronto,
Beloit, Detroit, or even Chicago.
It didn't matter where the road would go,
So long as I could avoid the undertow,
Of bell, book, and candle, I was pale and stale,
And needed to hit the blue, asphalt trail.

Each Spring these professors conjure to convene,
To careen on a trip they find serene,
To find new technologies as they teach,
Spreading the word as far as they can reach,
Satellite uplinks and microwave TV,
Both show promise to spread the word broadly,
And, the Internet shows much potential, too,
Both as a research and teaching tool.
Some professors have developed courses
On topics from zebras to antsy horses,

Beamed online via WEB sites with email,
Generating a letter grade, pass or fail.
My name's *Jose Roberto,* call me *Bob,*
Manning the van would be my actual job
To check the oil, gas the tank, and drive,
Taking us far beyond the Great Divide.
At the end of each narrated tale
The driver's opinion would prevail,
Commenting about each of the tales told,
While also keeping the van on the road.
I would introduce each storyteller
As a good old boy, a steady feller,
With no defamational slurs allowed
In this cantankerous, convivial crowd.

All eight men are professors, true blue,
T. Osprey Munsch
Recently completed graduate school;
Virgil Vulgate
Is an ancient linguist *par excellence,*
Classical Latin and Greek are his ambiance;
Buster White
Used to be an animal doctor,
Who left science for cowboy lore;
Lawrence Carrow
Teaches civil tort liability,
Legal ethics are his propensity;
Lupé de Vega
Is grounded in Hispano folklore,
Which he shares *con cariño y amor;*
Tommy Tornado
Was a former rock and roll idol
Who still jams a swinging recital;

Smokey Cloud
Professor of paleontology,
Is as Negroid-black as Muhammad Alí;
Lolo Sandec
Is a consummate artist, by heck,
Who never plays cards with a full deck.
Of the only female on this long trip,
She, too, would be introduced without slip,
As a good old boy, one of the steady gals,
After all, men are among her best pals.

Inger Johnson
Is a children's literature librarian,
And a fine, feminist contrarian.

We loaded up the van in pronto haste,
Strapping bags on rack, we'd no time to waste,
Tom's acoustic guitar was tied on top,
Easy to reach when we made a stop.
For seating, the profs were quick to decide
The positions for everyone on the ride,
Lucky for us, we had good old Lolo,
Who was willing to ride in the back row,
Inger was to ride shotgun, on the right side,
Beside the driver for most of the ride.

1

BUSTER BECKONS THE BEAT

Of a rootin' tootin' cowboy who goes wrong
By helping another poke mosey along,
Whereafter, we hear of tall men, there were three,
Who can't agree upon what they see,
Buster then torques as a tall tale sketcher
Twisting and turning a true Texas stretcher.

Bob: We're off! We're up and ready to go,
Full steam ahead to start our big show,
Buster White will be the first one to speak,
He just read some of his poems last week
To a raunchy, rough and rowdy crowd,
Who listened to him quietly enthralled.
Buster's a well-known cowboy poet,
So he'll do a good job, he won't blow it,
Buster, my man, we're counting on you
To set the tone for our riming review.

Buster: I reckon y'all can count on me,
No use frettin' the way our turns will be.
I was raised in Texas near San Angelo,
Where the mesquite and *cholla* cactus grow,
As a lad, I read the book of King James,
Learning most of its places and names,
Then, when I attended Texas A & M,
I was introduced to *the* Charles Darwin,
Who claimed the world evolved in gradual ways,
But King James said it only took six days.

Confused, I set the contradictions aside,
Knowing someday, someway they'd collide,
That's when I became a vet, a horse doctor,
But, I wasn't any good, I couldn't proctor
Which horses to let die and which to let be,
The dissonance was a mite too much for me.

Meantime, S. Omar Barker was my hero,
He taught me how to use cowboy lingo
To show cowboys are *vaqueros* at heart,
Most times, it's hard to tell them apart,
Some night when you got nothing better to do,
Read his book, *Ballads of the Buckaroo.*
I believe the Lord thinks like a cowboy,
And, sure-as-shoot, made this world to enjoy,
In cowboy poems, there's religion enough
Without getting snookered on heady stuff.
This here ballad is about an old friend,
Who got lassoed and hobbled by a trend.

The Beatnik Cowboy
Hanging around on Last Chance Street,
Cluttered with coffee shops and bars,
I happened to meet Cowboy Beat
With a little lady in leotards.

He was a sad critter to behold,
A hard luck story a mile long,
How he never fit the cowboy mold,
Nor could he sing a ridin' song.

I felt kinda sorry for him,
So I had a talk with my boss,

Who gave him work on condition
He wouldn't become a loss.

He never shaves, just raves,
"Dumb luck, that's all it is,
For the sucker that craves
To be more'n a fish."

Now he'd have a chance again
To save his hard luck soul,
By working from dawn to ten p.m.,
Showing he fit the cowboy mold.

Beat walks up the street with me,
Leaving the coffee shops and bars,
He's to live in co-o-o-ld reality,
Forsakin' the lady in leotards.

Last I heard, he was at the T. O. Ranch
Working into the cowboy mold,
Doin' his best, given the chance
To let cowboying take a'hold.

He never shaves, just raves,
"Dumb luck, that's all it is,
For the sucker that craves
To be more'n a fish."

A year later on Last Chance Street,
Sidewalk covered with snow and ice,
I crossed the path of Cowboy Beat,
Clinging to a lady really nice.

Had I seen her some place before?
I seemed to know that pretty smile,
It must'a been before the war,
I'll ask Beat in a little while.

I kept walking 'long my way,
Generally thinking about life,
About how each dog has his day—
Heck, man! That lady was my wife!

He never shaves, just raves,
"Dumb luck, that's all it is,
For the sucker that craves
To be more'n a fish."

What? Huh? I asked her how come
She was clinging to Cowboy Beat?
She said not a word, handed me a drum,
And left me standing in the street.

So now it's here that I stay,
Among the coffee shops and bars,
With some bongos I can't play,
And a lady in leotards.

Next time yer a'walking on ice,
And eager to help your fellow man,
Before you rush to give advice,
Take the coyote from the lamb.

He never shaves, just raves
"Dumb luck, that's all it is,
For the sucker that craves
To be more'n a fish."

Tom: Hey! That was cool and hep!
And, you told it with such pep.

Buster: Well, everthin's relative, dad-gummit,
It's accordin' to how you look at it,
Reminds me when I was taking in
The rocks and rills of Grand Canyon rim.

Three Tall Men

Three tall men stood at the Grand Canyon rim,
Gawking and gaping, taking its size all in,
One was an artist in every respect,
One, a preacher, one a cowboy, by heck.
The artist was struck by the Canyon's beauty,
Describing it in ways most folks don't see:
"Ah, the color, the hue, the symmetry,
The shapes, all these are important to me."
They all stood still, then up spoke the preacher:
"It's our Lord above, who's the great teacher,
Only He could create such a creature,
This Grand Canyon calls forth such piety,
It's the Lord's lesson to society."
They were awestruck and commenced to meditate,
Lost in thoughts only they could contemplate,
After many minutes had lapsed and passed,
They both turned to the cowboy and asked:
"Of this place of magnificent beauty,
Of more colors and hues than one can see,
Where every rim and rock and every tree
Blends together in splendid symmetry,
Tell us, of this Grand Canyon, what think thee?"
The 'poke brushed aside the grass with his boot,
Spitin', frownin', and frettin' to give a hoot,

He thought tough and rough. He thought long,
To give a slip-shod answer would be wrong,
'Cuz he wasn't used to deep thinking habits,
Not much goes into shooting deer and rabbits.
He wanted a true answer for these men,
Without sounding like a cackling hen,
So he scratched his head and said, "It depends
How you look at her bushes, boulders, and bends,
But I kin tell you how I see her now,
It'd be a helluva place to lose a cow."

All: Way to go!
    Dos-à-dos.

Inger: Buster, I find that I agree with you,
Relativisms are many points of view,
Once, I told some tales to Montana Crows
About White pioneers and all their woes.
The Crows said they didn't want gringo crap,
Meaning the tales were an ethnocentric trap
To justify the Army's determination
On a plan of Indian extermination.
At first, I thought they'd given me a bum rap,
Making me feel like a mighty flighty sap.

Tom: Torquay, Tuff-a-Nuff, and Sweet Lucy,
This chatter's getting loosey-goosey!

Bob: Tom, I'm supposed to do the talking,
And there you go a'squawking.

Buster: No need to fuss or debate,
Jist enjoy the tales, try to relate,

Think of me as a kind of sketcher
Of tall tales, like the Texas stretcher,
If you get my drift, so to speak,
Here's one I heard jist last week.

Ol' Boy Texas Jack

Most folks don't know about the jackalope,
A critter crossed with a prairie antelope
And a jack rabbit with long, floppy ears,
First spotted in Wyoming in bygone years.

You know you spotted one when you look-see
What appears to be a jackrabbit at tea,
Standing on hind legs, sporting floppy ears,
And the antelope's pronghorns—not a deer's.
Consider yourself lucky to spy one,
They're private and don't come out to sun,
They don't herd with antelope or rabbits,
And don't cotton game-hunter's habits.
Last winter I spent all of three *noches,*
Though it felt like a week in Nacogdoches,
Where I learned of a similar critter
From a cowboy claimed he was Tex Ritter:
In 1829, between Poth and Polk,
George McLean claimed he spied a jackalope,
And while he was branded a half-pint liar,
Cowboys on the trail reported a choir

Of jackalopes that echoed a cowboy's song
When cowboys sang to the herds all night long.
The cowboys said jackalopes sang fair as a lark
Before thunderstorms when the sky was dark,

And though jackalopes warbled like a fowl,
They didn't pack up like coyotes to howl.

Now, Texans claim many species of fauna,
Such as armadillos on marijuana,
Yellow-dog Democrats, digital drovers,
Mammoth mosquitoes and lunar land rovers,
Jumbo shrimp crimped in Corpus Christi Bay,
Dust devils served in dust bowls on a good day,
When you can be in mud up to your hips
And be blasted with dust balls in the lips.
So I don't dispute the Texas jackalope
That's changed century-old customs to cope,
Because the true Texas jackalope sports
Deer antlers, deer hooves, deer ears, and comports
With drugstore cowboys, barrel bulls, hot dogs,
Coffee connoisseurs, and Harley hogs.
The Texas critter would best be called "Jack Deer,"
Not to be mistaken for *the* "John Deere,"
Also a well-known critter of Texas
As common as pickups and the *Lexus.*
I reckon there's no call to dispute
The fact of ol' boy Jack. He don't pollute
When he lets go gas near a Texas town,
Locals bottle and sell it to the British Crown,
Green Party candidates, Republicans,
Dixiecrats, Democrats, fathers and sons.
Come to think of it, I admire Jack
And wouldn't be scared to turn my back

For fear he'd attack, or dump a load,
He's no yellow-bellied horny toad.

Bob: Buster, you clearly set the tone,
Allowing everyone else to hone,
To sharpen what they do the best
As we drive along to the west.

Maybe, it's time to stop for gas
Before we cross the Fourth of July Pass?

All: Yep! Sure! Why not? Take time for the pot.

2

VIRGIL VENTURES TO HELL AND BACK

Virgil ventures into a professor's hell,
Wherein committee meetings are the eternal cell,
Verily, Virgil ponders on rabbits and fates,
When jackrabbits take on business traits,
Ending by asking: why build a highway bridge,
Simply to crossover the road, ridge-to-ridge?
Or, is there a higher intent in mind
Bridge builders dare us to seek and find?

Bob: We are honored to have here among us,
A classical, cutting-edge thesaurus,
He's our own Dr. Virgil Vulgate,
A scholar who would never titillate
With his expansive tomes of Latin roots,
Campy cognates, and lexical off-shoots.
Virgil just finished a ten-volume series
On the Latin used in the Pyrenees,
And, if the Vandals ever dare come back,
They would have, at least, ten volumes to sack!
Virgil, we're anxiously awaiting,
Nay, we're tepidly anticipating
Your ballad will be upright recondite,
And its meter will be squeaky-clean tight.

Virgil: Your doggerel makes me up-chuck and gag,
Good thing I brought a plastic, doggie bag,
Heavens, with an introduction like that,
Full of malarkey, rot-gut and clap-trap,

It's a wonder anybody cares
About the state of academic affairs.

Inger: Yes siree, Bob, you were crass,
Just like a braying jackass,
E-haw! E-haw! How did you bray
While throwing jibes his way,
To Latin, Virgil gave his life,
Even loves it more than his wife.

Buster: Let's not get angry or uptight,
Would you drive at night with no light?
Would you respect a dog with no bite?
What's a driver without a fight?

Virgil: Thank you, colleagues, for helping me subdue,
Some of the meaner aspects of Bob's review,
But, let's not forget our original rule,
Bob is allowed to make a comment or two
Before I present my ballad to you.

Hell Canyon Campus

I took a walk one hot and windy day,
And atop a canyon wall I rested,
When all at once I heard the doleful bay
Of wretched souls, forlorn and detested.

For down yonder on the Hell Canyon floor
Was the rubble of a decaying campus,
All that remained was the frame of Old Main door,
Inscribed: "All ye who enter must seek consensus."

What hokus pokus did the line relate,
Scribed over the door of Hell Canyon campus?
I ran down the draw at a heartbreak rate
To inspect first-hand this gloomy locus.

Before Old Main frame thrust a promenade,
Where novices were hastened to follow,
I joined a cloister in solemn parade,
Their hair was sallow gray, their eyes aglow.

Down,
      down,
            the promenade dropped
And swallowed us
Down an escalator into the ground,
Where a multiplex of rooms was hollowed,
Equipt with chairs and tables, square and round.

Professors were shuffling from room to room,
Their breaths were hot, their tongues afire,
Their sallow faces gaunt and full of gloom—
Hmm. There were no women in the pyre.

A bolt of wonderment pierced my praxis,
As I pondered the mournful cries:
"All ye who enter must seek consensus,
And Dean L. Devil breaks the ties."

I walked the hall of the underground mall,
Peering in the rooms as I passed along,
Noting the ho-hum-drum of each roll call
And the pervasive fear of being wrong.

The Executive Committee was in full stride,
They cussed and discussed, my did they ever curse,
They were charged to decide how to decide,
To be or not to be, which was the worse?

Prideful professors grieved to pose queries,
To wit, "who evaluates the Devil Dean?"
They prayed to the Committee-on-Committees
To form a committee to check the scene.

Few vied for the Shared Governance Committee,
Where Hitler and Stalin forged an alliance,
Deputizing Professor Simon Legree
To help Dean L. Devil enforce compliance.

Most eschewed the Committee on Reports,
For once a report was written, it spawned
The need to write more reports as retorts,
To the first reports, so it went on and on.

A jolt of fear ran through my senses,
I shivered in sweat at the mournful cries:
"All ye who enter must seek consensus,
And Dean L. Devil breaks the ties."

As for the Committee on Diversity,
Varying views were viciously vilified,
To protect the perpetuation of perversity
All words of truth and justice were sillified.

The Committee on Tenure was in contention,
Disputing its retention and tenure,

Dean L. Devil redressed the pretension:
"You're tenured to meet in committee forever!"

Oh, my! Not all professors had tongues afire,
Quite a few had lips that were zippered shut,
But their hands and heads were free to gyre,
To make motions of aye and nay in rebut.

Shaking and dropping my defenses,
I shuttered at the mournful cries:
"All ye who enter must seek consensus,
And Dean L. Devil breaks the ties."

The fear that was in me would not decease,
Ah, me! There was nothing to stem my strife,
So I sought the advice of Socrates,
Who rebuked: "Young man, get a life!"

"But, what became of the life of the mind,"
I asked, "there's got to be a better place,
Than rooms where miserable men think on hind,
And ideas are killed without a trace?"

"It's big ideas you want? Come with me,"
Socrates signaled, "down this steel stairwell,
To the nuclear furnace room where you'll see
Ideas stoking the fires of hell."

Socrates led down the steel stairwell,
Which was glowing pink and smelled of rubber,
By the rank smell of burnt soles, I could tell,
Many had tread here, one time or other.

"Before I open the door," Socrates warned,
"Prepare yourself for a vision very scary,
Here all the burned-out professors," he mourned,
"Must masticate, meditate and make merry.

For sabbaticals they proffer to go
To this fiery furnace room of untold rune,
Where they come and go talking of Leonardo
While slurping syllogisms from a spoon.

You'll see Muckers, faces skewed in puckers,
They've defied the charge of their committee,
Naked and without gown, these poor suckers
Spend their leave chanting the word *conformity*."

A moment of truth prodded my haunches,
I couldn't elude the mournful cries:
"All ye who enter must seek consensus,
And Dean L. Devil breaks the ties."

Socrates opened the door. We were seared
By the blast of hot air that rushed past,
Everyone in the radiant room appeared
To glow and effuse a crimson pink caste.

They were all there: the Mucker, the Buckster,
And the Pragmatists who were playing pool,
The Canonites opposed to Multiculture,
And the Unionists who were plotting a coup.

Emeriti were dusting-off the Great Books
Written more than a millennium ago,

And judging by their clean and crispy looks,
Hadn't been read over a century or so.

The strangest consortium of them all
Were the Big Bangers and the Nihilists,
Blaming the Devil Dean for the Great Fall
And the rise of Christian Existentialists.

By now I was grasping for my nexus
To dispel the wretched mournful cries:
"All ye who enter must seek consensus,
And Dean L. Devil breaks the ties."

"I can tell by the furrowed frowns on your face,"
Socrates decried, "You're going down fast,
As you have no taste for our ponderous pace
To fossilize ideas into a cast.

If you don't change your life, I fear,
You'll be like us in search of quorum,
From meeting to meeting without cheer,
And a furnace room for finding forum."

I bolted out the room! Up the staircase!
Dashing swiftly past each committee room,
I saw at each place my zipper-lipped face,
Muted, muzzled, unable to commune.

As I fled the maw of Hell Canyon campus,
I heard the echoes of the mournful cries:
"All ye who enter must seek consensus,
And Dean L. Devil breaks the ties."

Bob: Now, Virgil, I mean this most sincerely,
Your Hell Canyon story hit me dearly,
You know I'm a novice graduate student,
And your tale makes me ask if it's prudent
To study to join the professor's race,
For tenure, promotion, and office space.

T. Osprey: What with the committee meeting wails,
I best stop spinning bogus fishing tales.

Lolo: Committee meetings would be sheer hell
As ends in themselves. They're supposed to be
A means to an end, a process to gel
Shared governance at the university.
Granted some faculty get carried away,
Using the meetings to hear themselves talk,
Some administrators use them as a way
To hold sway on the process, ad hoc.

Lawrence: *'Shared governance'* is a slippery concept,
Based on a flawed, political precept.
When there's talk of shared governance,
Be wary of prior deals and covenants,
For when it comes down to sharing power,
You might presume to climb a greasy tower,
From the start, you're on a dubious trip,
When you try to climb, you can't even grip.
People who have power don't care to share,
Like sharing berries with a bear.

Inger: Hell Canyon College should trip an alarm
About the good old boy's seductive charm,

Stand your vigil ready and alert,
Don't mess around with the women or flirt,
Let them profess like you, or you'll be hurt,
You know! They've ideas to assert.

T. Osprey: Did'ja notice no women down there?
Somehow, that fact appears to be unfair,
Yet, if we've excluded them from the workplace,
We can't expect them to join us in the fireplace.

Buster: Boy, howdy! All this here is jim-dandy,
Anybody have an old cowboy song-book handy?
Virgil's poem copies the *Ghost Riders* song,
Only the song isn't nearly half as long.

Lolo: It's also based on one of Dante's best works,
Of the dreadful idea that haunts and lurks—
Are there variegated versions of hell
That each of us selects to make, as well?

Virgil: That reminds me of another tale
Of our tiny trip across the vale.

The Jumping Jack

One night as I drove down Beartooth Pass,
I spied jack rabbits chomping on the grass,
Cloistered in small groups on the shoulders,
Busy eating grass between the boulders.

One jack jumped from his group onto the road,
Hopping as though he had cargoes to load,
Meetings to attend, he was running late,
Whatever, he took on a business-like trait

As he hopped in a hurried, jagged line,
Like he had important clients to wine.
I imagined him in a Brooks Brothers suit,
Briskly bustling down a street in hot pursuit
To foreclose a contract, like Donald Trump,
Then, he zigzagged into my lane and thump!
The car hit him head-on with its heavy grill,
And for a quick moment I felt a chill,
Turning sharply, I had swerved to miss him
As the car careened on a dangerous mission,
A few feet further down on the shoulder
Would've smashed us into a big boulder,
Or, even worse, plunged us down the switchback,
So why did I swerve to miss the jumping jack?

Lolo: I can see swerving to try to miss a deer,
Or an ambling Amish wagon from the rear,
But getting killed just to miss a jumping jack
Is not a very good plan of attack.

Virgil: Lucky, I jerked the car back on the road
While my mind sprang and spun in overload,
For I'd just read about some kids who died,
They swerved to miss a deer and not collide,
When they ran off the road, they hit a huge rock
That instantly killed them all…stopped their clock.

Lawrence: You're right to ponder and question,
But for Bob, I have a practical suggestion,
So long as you're driving, and we're in this van,
Don't swerve, dammit! Miss the rabbit if you can,
But if you hit it, well, it's just too late,
You were meant to be in its plan of fate.

Buster: Whoa! We're gittin' downright myopic,
High time we changed the topic,
Say-hey, y'all, not just our top drover,
Did'ja count the bridges that crossover?

T. Osprey: More bridges 'an a stringer with fish on it,
When you've live-baited beyond your limit.

Lawrence: Interstates were built on 'eminent domain,'
Taking right-of-way over anybody's claim,
And though the road took its own right-of-way,
It had to provide everybody leeway,

That is, folks must have access to their land,
Be it good topsoil or worthless sand.
Building bridges was the easy solution
For access, though a costly resolution.

Virgil: Talk of the many bridges reminds me
Of trips when we drove the family
To visit Vesta's folks west of St. Paul,
All the way on Interstates, a long haul.

Begetting Bridges

It was a game we played, Vesta and I
With the kids as we drove the Interstates,
Missoula to St. Paul under the big sky,
Undulating pastures via three states,

Fields of milo, corn, barley, and sunflowers,
With stops at a rest area or gas station,
A tedious trip with plenty of hours
To tug and stretch the imagination.

Why does the bridge crossover? Why was it built?
What mysterious places does it take
People trekking the Great Plains patch-quilt
Of black hills, badlands, and gravel pit lakes?

Does the bridge lead to a toy town for kids,
Like Bedrock City with its games and rides,
Where you can stride a dino-mobile on skids,
Or finger-paint pictures on dino-hides?
Does the bridge lead to a dinosaur's grave,
Ancient swamps where it was buried and died,
Firmly fossilized bits of bones to save
A permanent log of where it once thrived?

Does it lead to a working ranch where cowboys
Drive ATVs to check and mend fences,
Roundup cows with dirt bikes, other big-boy-toys,
Download Buster White as a preference,
But for a reference, they use other tools:
Computer spread sheets and the Internet
To keep tight track of the herd's gene pools,
The onset of allergies, or a birth defect.

Does it lead to our nation's enshrined dome,
Mt. Rushmore where heads of Presidents burst
From stone outcroppings, and buffalo roam
On ridges that belonged to the Sioux first?
Suppose it leads to a corporate farm
Where Jolly Green Giants stand guard

Over giant green machines that beep alarm
To avoid backing over hens in the yard?
Maybe the bridge doesn't lead anywhere,
Built by a self-serving chief engineer

To give his brother a private crossover,
A political pork barrel, as it were?
Or, maybe it doesn't go anywhere now,
But will someday rise to the occasion,
Perhaps a town will grow to it somehow,
Sprouting a diner, motel, and gas station?

Lawrence: A bridge should be a smooth connection,
With no bumps on the lips of either side,
Spanning highways, chasms, creeks, or canyon,
Advancing people on their journey's ride.

Lupe: I'd like to think teaching does just that,
Stretching students from one point to the next,
Flexing their faculties to fathom the gap,
And move on, advancing their curious quest.

Buster: Me-oh-my! Reach for the sky! I declare,
You touted cowboys with modern hardware.

Virgil: Just because I teach about ancient tomes,
Doesn't mean I live in Roman catacombs.

Bob: I don't mean to bug you so,
But, there's something you should know,
The miles ahead are still a long way to go,
So, I'll tank-up on coffee and not eat a bite,
That way, I'll be able to drive all through the night.

Inger: If you tank-up on coffee, what you mean,
You'll have to stop all night to ventilate your spleen.

T. Osprey: Among the advantages of being a man,
　　　　　We can stop anywhere to stand to use the can.

Inger: An advantage to being male?
　　　　You'll not take it beyond the pale.

Virgil: Me thinks the lovely lady doth protest,
　　　　For she can't enter the pissing contest.

Buster: For me, I soon get there just as fast as we can,
　　　　We'll get our forty winks sitting in this here van.

Lawrence: As for me, I sure would like to catnap,
　　　　But Bob, how's your reading of the map?

Bob: Walla Walla will be our next pit stop,
To fill her up with gas, groceries, and pop,
Don't worry about your corns or bunions,
You won't have to walk far for good onions,
Because in the Walla Walla Valley,
The onions are as sweet as can be.

Lolo: Thanks for the lesson on pop and grocery,
Now, kindly stick to the geography.

Bob: From Walla Walla it's a barren ride,
Good thing it's getting late, and we can slide
Through the dark across Oregon to Burns,
So take care, now, of your bodily concerns.

Then, we continue to tiny Alturas,
Where we might be able to stop for gas,

If not, it's to Redding or Sacramento,
We'll have to play it by ear, as we go.

Professors, I'm stopping at Walla Walla,
Make the most of it, don't whine and holla!....

We didn't stay in Walla Walla too long,
Nor buy any onions to take along.
As we traversed Oregon's eastern slope,
All I thought of was Matt Dillon in *Gunsmoke*,
How the west is not what it used to be,
With buffalo as far as you can see,
Unless you count as buffalo, the llama,
Or that silly bird, *como se yama?*
The ostrich, with the neck of a tea pot,
And a pea brain no larger than a dot.
South of Burns, we watched the night
Slip a cover over the dimming daylight,
In the western big sky, a wisp of a cloud
Faded into the unfolding nightly shroud,
Up high, a crooked line of geese etched the sky,
Drafting each other on their northern ply.
Would they land to eat and bed for the night,
Or persist, using stars to guide their flight?
Or are they guided by a magnetic dole
That directs them toward the North Pole?

3

LUPE DIGS DEEP INTO TRADITION

Of the luckless Rose Corona
A.K.A. the Wailing Woman, La Llorona,
Of Don Carlo and the hey-diddle-diddle
That put sparks in his eyes and fiddle,
Then, Levi Leyba gives faith healing all he's got
And sells his life for a chicken in the pot,
Last, an angel angles to guard kids on strolls,
But is troubled to hunt down passed-on souls.

Bob: Lupe de Vega tells me to cut short
An introduction of any sort,
He has some comments that need to be said,
Before he pushes full-bore ahead.

Lupe: Wherever *Los Mejicanos* are found,
Their mythic, legendary characters abound.
You might hear a *cuento* in Nebraska,
Or much further north in Alaska,
You might hear a *cuento* in Laredo, Texas,
Where *La Bruja* has put many of her hexes,
You might hear a *cuento* in sunny San Diego,
Where *La Curandera* works in the Stop-n-Go,
You might hear a *cuento* in Ohio,
Where the *campesinos* pick tomato.

A *cuento* tells what these characters have done
En todo los pueblos under the Aztec sun,
You'll hear of *La Curandera,* the faith-healer,
Of *La Bruja* the witch, the Devil's Dealer,

And of the Angel of Death, *La Muerte,*
Como el dicho, no *hay quien escape,*
But, most of all, you'll hear of *La Llorona,*
Who is the most tragic of all the persona.
In *todos los pueblos,* she takes a different name,
That she's the Wailing Woman remains the same,
She's forsaken to live *solita*…alone,
Without children or a cozy home of her own.
Here is one such sad *cuento* of *La Llorona,*
Better known as Rose Corona.

La Llorona **Rose Corona**

Narciso was called 'rooster,' or *gallo,*
Who deflowered girls wherever he'd go,
Thus with Rose, he made love to her
With abandon only he could confer.
Nine months pass. Rose was heavy with child
And found her tender love reviled,
Spurned by Narciso, a dishonorable man,
Who wouldn't consent to a wedding bann.
In fact, he denied knowledge of the child,
Insisting Rose give birth in the wild.
The day came. She walked to the Rio Grande
With a *curandera* who laid-on a healing hand,
Helping, when her water broke, to scrub and clean,
Burying the placenta in soil near the scene.
(When it rains, it pours, giving cause to mourn,
Rose's blameless baby boy was stillborn.)

Quickly, the curandera acted
Before the dead child exacted
Too much sorrow from Rose,
She ripped strips of cloth from her clothes,

Found a fallen tree trunk in a bog,
Then tied the boy to the log.
They carried log and boy through the sedge
Of bramble bushes to the river's edge,
Shoved the child onto the bobbing stream,
Watching till he barely could be seen
Drifting toward the bank where the river bent,
Down...down river he drifted on the current,
Floating...floating...floating.
Wedging on an overhang, soggy and dank,
Cottonwood roots dangled over the bank,
Growing down-and-around the log and boy,
Scooping them into the tree, to Rose's joy,
Entombing the boy in the trunk of the tree,
Sealing his fate for eternity.

The deed done, Rose returned to Narciso
To seek his support and share her woe.
She told of their stillborn love child
Floating down the river running wild,
How the cottonwood extended its shoots Entombing
the boy in its dangling roots.
Then, she quoted *Exodus, Chapter Twenty-Two*,
To give guidance to what Narciso should do:
"If a man entice a maid that he is not betrothed,
And lie with her,
He should surely endow her to be his wife."
Presto! Just like that, Narciso balked,
Swearing, cursing, pacing while he talked
Of the dead child floating on the raft

As proof-positive Rose practiced witchcraft,
Quoting same Book and Chapter,
Here's what he had to give,

Verse 18: "Thou shalt not suffer a witch to live."
(Of all that's in Heaven and Earth, one thing is sure,
Even the Devil can quote Scripture.)

He called a meeting of the workers on the ranch,
By now, Rose knew she didn't have a chance,
The workers would back their low-down boss,
Casting the dice against her—a capricious toss.
The meeting convened in Narcisco's courtyard manor,
Which was landscaped in a Southwestern manner.
For Rose there would be a trial by fire,
Were she innocent, she'd survive the burning pyre.

Narciso turned to the cringing, kowtowed crowd,
Who cowered and agreed, the trial was allowed,
Rose was tied to a dead-standing tree
And dry branches were piled in faggots of three.
The fire lit. Rose started to wail,
Piercing *la gente's* ears on a high, harmonic scale:
"*Wa-eeee-o-o-o-o-o,*
Yo soy la novia de Nar-ci-so-o-o-o,
Wa-eeee-o-o-o-o-o,
Yo soy la novia de Nar-ci-so-o-o-o-o-o-o-o-o-o....."
The flame consumed her and the dead-tree,
Oh, misery, pain and agony

None can describe. Nor will I try,
Her spirit lifted into the sky,
Burning body crumpled, still a-flame—
Narciso proclaimed, "witchcraft was to blame."
Two years pass. Narciso at the prime of life,
Announced he would soon take a wife
At a festive wedding held in the courtyard outside

To unite him with a Spanish bride.
All workers and families were invited to come,
To partake in the gay festivities and fun,
A priest was procured; banns were announced,
So claims on the union could be made or renounced.
The wedding morning was bright and clear
As workers and families gathered in good cheer,
The courtyard was circled with tables decked in food,
Good eats and wines to enhance the mood.

A *musico* played many a toe-tapping tune,
Evoking a sound so smooth you could swoon,
I can say this crowd was much gayer and higher
Than the one who burned Rose on the pyre
In this self-same courtyard almost two years ago,
When Rose was staked and torched by Narciso.
Padre Palaver called the festive crowd to order,
Asking them to stand around the courtyard border,
The groom and his party would stand in the middle
While the bride approached at the sound of the fiddle,
Marching from the *casa grande* to mid-court,
Where exchange of vows and rings would comport.
By now, it was a mellow summer afternoon
With a balmy breeze blowing a tacit tune,
The weather so fine one couldn't disparage,
Superbly splendid for a summer marriage.

The fiddler played, after he rosined-up his bow,
Eking out a tender tune, velvet smooth and slow,
The bride marched slowly up the flowered path
When a bellowing thunder rolled in her aftermath—
Kerpop! Out of the blue, a lightning struck,
Splitting a cottonwood—a puny puck!

Folks standing by the stricken tree, jumped away,
A bit shaken. None were hurt, all okay.
The treetop toppled, crashing into other trees,
Without spreading sparks in the balmy breeze,
The split tree trunk glowed as a burning ember,
But, there were no flames anyone can remember.
From within the split tree,
                    children came sprawling,
All abandoned by Narciso, crawling
To join the once happy, festive crowd,
Who now appeared to be wearing a purple shroud.
From the trunk, a spirit slipped out in a slide,
Rose Corona dressed as a bride,

Wearing a silken white, close-fitting wedding gown,
Cut to fit her snugly from the shoulders down,
Neckline embroidered with fine golden thread
And a laurel of fresh daisies on her head.
From the waistline, the gown was cut to hang full,
Draping in full folds at her feet, and sides, too,
An ample train flowed down-and-back about five feet,
Carried by Narciso's children dressed trim and neat.

There she hovered:
        a stunning bride with long, black hair,
Eyes and face aglow, radiant and debonair,
Never was such a lovely apparition seen
Emerging from the ashes of a burning scene.
Like a hummingbird gliding on gossamer wings,
She flitted back and forth, inspecting all things,
After all, this was to be her wedding day,
Custom dictates she would have much to say

About the flower arrangements and dress attire
As well as the music played by fiddler or choir.
When she saw it was Don Carlo fiddling so quick,
She was immensely pleased. He was her pick.

Gliding around and about with agility,
She floated in-and-out the crowd so all could see
The silken beauty of her gown and its long train,
While Don Carlo played a rueful refrain.
Rose levitated to Narciso's side
To take her rightful place as his eternal bride,
The children, carrying her train, levitated too,
Without treading on earth, they were a floating crew.
Then Rose grabbed Narciso by the hand
As she shouted to the terrific one-man band,
To strike up some swinging, toe-tapping tunes,
To dance with Narciso before he swoons:
"¡ *Corridos y polkas, por favor* !"
Don Carlo work up a jumpy toe-tapper,
As she took the lead, Narciso wasn't too dapper,

She twirled him in broad sweeps around the courtyard,
Making the macabre dance look easy, not too hard.
¡*O, si*, the agile children who carried the train,
Swept right along with the dancers without a strain.
The dance ended. Narciso a trembling wretch,
Not an ounce of gall or gumption could he fetch,
For he had burned Rose into the ground,
And here she was levitating, dancing around,
Wailing in a chilly keen so *la gente* could hear,
Casting fear and anxiety, though she meant to cheer:
"*Wa-eeee-o-o-o-o-o, wa-eeee-o-o-o-o-o,*
Yo soy la novia de Narciso."

Pandemonium erupted! *Gente* ran here and there
In utter chaos, knocking down tables and chair,
Grabbing their churlish children and sputtering spouses,
They hied away to hide in their humble houses,
Even Narciso's mortal bride left him high and dry
To lie with a ghostly bride whom he'd caused to die.
The mortal bride retreated, reeling in reverse,
Escaping a marriage made in hell, and worse,
To share the wedding bed with his phantom wife,
Who had been spurned and burned, robbed of life.
This ends the terrible tale of deceit and woe,
Of resplendent Rose and her grudging *gallo*.

Lolo: Ah, a sad, sad tale of old
That should be told and retold.

Lupe: The gentleman in the tale who tore my heart
Was the fiddler who so ably plied his part.

The Fiddler

Don Carlo, he was called out of respect
For his demeanor and gentle aspect,
Blind as a bat, the good *Don* could not see,
Which is why he played the fiddle for a fee,
As he played, he passed his hat in the crowd,
So folks could pitch-in as they were endowed.

One Saturday night as he played in a bar,
Two young men flared-up and started to spar,
Somehow, *Don* Carlo got caught in the middle
Of the fight and the fighters' hey-diddle-diddle.

Thud! One socked, knocked him to the ground,
Forcing a fast stop to his winsome sound,
Everyone in the bar commenced to shout,
Accosting the young men, chewing them out,
For one of them had socked Carlo too hard,
Stopping the music of the blind bard.
The young men pulled *Don* Carlo to his feet,
Apologizing for their brutish conceit.
"*Pues, no le hace,*" Don Carlo replied,
"Your sock gave me the light I'd been denied,
I saw stars when you punched me straight away,
Another punch might've brought the light of day.
Though I got caught in your hey-diddle-diddle,
Look! No harm's come to my trusty fiddle,
And I don't care to demand redress,
Your lucky punch brought light for egress."

Lupe: Don Carlo always took a bright outlook,
Though he'd hardly seen light or read a book,
He was a good man, who never did wrong,
For a mere dime, he'd fiddle a jig or song.
He could tell tales with a bit of a bite,
Though he told them kindly without spite.
Sadly, no one knows what became of the bard,
Last seen, he was loafing in his backyard,
A freakish fire burned his shack to the ground,
And none of his personal things could be found,
Except the charred remains of his fiddle,
For pooff! *Don* Carlo was gone with the flame
Without sign of leaving by foot or train,
But without his fiddle, would he be able
To pay the rent and put food on his table?

Tom: Don Carlo could've rosined in our shop
To play first fiddle when we dug the bop.

Bob: As for Rose's tale, we all know
In each of us, there's a Narciso.

Inger: Say, hey! What do you mean '*us*,' young man?
Feel for Rose, if you can.

Bob: Okay! Okay! Get off your high horse,
So Lupe's tales can run their course.

Lupe: The *curandera o curandero*,
Assists poor people burdened with woe.
It's the art of faith healing, and then some,
Prayers, herbs, and oils in combination
Are used to help *gente* when despair takes a toll,
In accordance with the *Holy Scroll,*
So says *James,* Chapter Five, Verse Fourteen:
"Is one of you ill? He should send for the elders
To pray over him and anoint him with oils…
The prayer offered in faith will save the sick man."
To cure the desperate *gente*, the *viejos* say,
They must be imbued *con la santa fé,*
That is to say, they must have faith in God,
Who created them from water and sod,
Without faith, the *viejos* say, they can't go far,
Sin la santa fé, mud is all they are.
Curanderas treat ailments of the soul,
Helping *los desguanzados* to be full and whole.

As for casting out hexes, spells and germs,
And many other bodily concerns,

The *curandera* works on several layers,
Depending on *yuerba buena* and prayers,
Sometimes, she uses ointments and oils,
Taken from the plants of sundry soils.
La Curandera is put to high use,
Admittedly at times, the cause of abuse,

But, when there are no doctors to be found,
A *curandera* is sure to make her round.
Both men and women are called up to serve,
To do the work of the Master, to preserve
The sanctity of the Word of the Lord,
In the absence of a medical board.
Some serve as midwives, or *las parteras,*
Others serve as masseuses, *las sobadoras,*
Some dispense herbs and spices, *los yeberos,*
Others purge spells and hexes, *los brujos,*
Some serve as mediums to commune with the dead,
Inducing trances out of body and head.

This tale is of a man who lends a good ear,
Listening to tales of woe and giving cheer,
While he does *gente* some good along the way,
With plump chickens, he gets carried away.

You'll Not Eat at the Table Today
Levi Leyba was poor as a church mouse,
Unaccustomed to eating pheasant and grouse,
Thus, he connived to steal a plucky, plump hen
From within his rich neighbor's chicken pen.

Boldly, he walked into the chicken coop
And grabbed a plump hen without much pursuit,

Gripping her firmly by the legs and neck
So she couldn't run away or peck,
Still, she jabbered and cackled quite a storm,
Abusing Levi with cackling scorn.

He took the hen home to Josie, his wife
Who shared the burdens of their lean life.
She was so happy to see such a hen,
She sang sappy songs, fourscore and ten,
But, not before she took the hen outside,
Chopping off her head without breaking stride,
Causing the hen's head to drop to the ground,
While the hen ran in circles, round-and-round,

With blood spurting from her neck like a geyser,
When thud! She hit a tree, none the wiser,
Falling on her side, her toes a'twitching,
Clasping, grasping as though they were itching.

Josie gaily gripped the expiring hen
And carried her back into their dingy den,
To soak her in warm water, good and wet
And pluck her clean at one steady set.
Josie plucked the hen with such relish,
That there's no need for me to embellish.
Before long, the hen was plucked and ready
To bake in the cookstove oven, warm and steady.
Heart, liver, and gizzard were finely ground
With bread, eggs, and any food scraps around
The kitchen table that might go to waste,
To spice up the stuffing, according to taste.

Of course, the entrails were discarded
Before baking preparations were started.
As the hen baked, aromas commenced to crawl,

Wending out the oven and along the wall,
Floating freely over the dirt floor,
Creeping out the house through cracks in the door,
Drifting down the lane, attracting strangers
Who weren't shy to beg at Levi's chambers.

First to beg was Padre Palaver, the priest,
Whose mooching was dignified none the least,
He begged Levi for a taste of the hen,
Claiming he hadn't eaten since who knows when.
Yet, from the looks of his velvet cloak, one could see
He'd not kept a vow of poverty.

Levi objected, speaking his mind quite plain:
"¡*Que carajo*! You favor the rich and vain,
And don't care for *los pobres* who labor,
Why don't you beg from my *rico* neighbor?
I hate to break the news to you this way,
But, you'll not eat at the table today."

Next, a Protestant clergy came a'knocking,
Smelling the hen as he was a'walking,
He, too, begged Levi for a morsel bite,
Presuming a posture polite and contrite.
Again, Levi rebuffed the Man of God
For treating poor *peónes* like clumps of sod:
"No!" He pledged, "I won't give you a meal,
Porque you give *los pobres* a raw deal,
I hate to break the news to you this way,
But, you'll not eat at the table today."

The third stranger brought good luck, *buena suerte*,
For it was none other than *La Muerte*,
La comadre Sebastiana, also her name
Which adds affection to her fame.

Yes, at the door, it was the Angel of Death
Who was thirsty, hungry, and out of breath,
She assured Levi that her only request
Was to get a small bite to eat and to rest.

"¡*Entre*!" Levi beckoned, "come in for a meal,
For you give the rich and poor a fair deal,
La Muerte, you're one of God's greatest creatures,
For fairness in death is one of your features,
You treat the rich and poor souls much the same,
No man can stop his death with wealth or fame,
Rich or poor cannot escape La Muerte,
Como el dicho, no hay quien escape."

Josie sat La Muerte at the table,
Laying out a meal as she was able.
While La Muerte broke bread and ate the food,
Levi fell into a talkative mood,
Allowing that his was a humble life
Living in a shanty with a good wife:
"Heaven knows! An abiding faith in God
Is what keeps me from thinking like a clod,
Pero, you should know that I had to steal
The very food you're having for a meal."

La Muerte observed, "Hell would be a full lot
If We caught all poor men who stole for their pot,
But, our Father takes a much higher view,
Judging each for the over-all good they do,
That is, He takes a posture of wink and nod,
One of the best traits of our Lord the God.
Levi y Josie, you have treated me well,
And by your simple piety I can tell
That you are *muy buena gente de fé,*

Who helped me in my time of hunger and *sed*.
And so, I will explain though it's late at night
How to use your faith to make things right.

Levi, rather than being a leghorn-stealer,
You should try being a faith healer,
The satisfaction from curing is high,
And the salary is enough to get by.
When the despairing *gente* call on you,
Here are the simple rituals you should do:
Give a good ear. Listen to their tales of woe,
For many of them have a rough row to hoe,
With patience, learn to discern the woe they stow,
But remind them they will reap what they sow,
As they will be judged on the good they do,
Which they should, then, diligently pursue.
Now, it's time to culminate the rite
By lighting two candles in plain sight
For the cool nights and warm days given to us,
To do as we will, to rejoice or fuss.
The candles burn to remind us night and day
That life is short, and we have much to say
About how we feel as we wend our way
Across the lonesome valley, where we must go
Without knowing what the trip holds in stow.

When called to someone's bedside, shack or manor,
I will signal you in this simple manner:
If you see me standing at the foot of the bed,
You'll know it's okay to cure, to go ahead,
But, if you see me standing at the headboard,

You'll know it's time to give this soul to the Lord.
My image will be only for you to see,

A secret kept between you and me."
Completing her instructions, La Muerte left,
Leaving Levi to hurry, hustle, and heft,
To confer with the *viejos*, to learn their lore,
To discover what herbs they'd used before,
Such as brewing hot, soothing soups and teas,
From *la yerba buena* and leaves of trees.
Not long, and *gente* throughout the *pueblos*
Called on Levi to forestall *velorios*,
To cure them of their maladies and despair,
Or, at times, to remove a ball of hair
By using kerosene and turpentine,
Such a gross procedure that I decline
To describe how Levi purged the ball of hair
From people's *tripas* without a rip or tear,
(Always, La Muerte appeared at a bed board,
To signal to Levi the will of the Lord.)
Levi and Josie were flying high,
With Levi curing at most every try,
And though folks didn't always pay up-front,
Each was grateful for Levi's stealthy stunt,
Reimbursing him with cash or in-kind,
With a cut of beef or a porker's hind.
La Muerte would signal him, to be sure, Whenever he
was beckoned to cure,
So Levi would know just how to act,
Either to cure or state as a fact:
"I'm sorry, but the Lord is calling you,
And there's nothing that anyone can do."

Levi took on ailments *con mucho gusto,*
Even purging *tiricia y susto,*
With spices and herbs of purgative power
That were imbibed by brews, sweet and sour,

He even cured a monk who had *susto* bad,
So bad, the monk had gone stark, raving mad.
Once, when Bernardo the monk was translating,
He fell into deep thought, contemplating

An old, musty book of forgotten lore,
That no one, other than him, had read before.
He got to thinking, "why not claim the old tome
As a book he'd written as one of his own?
Maybe, just maybe, he'd be canonized
Among the Great Saints?" Then he realized
That plagiarism, the scholar's sin of pride,
Had crept beneath his intellectual hide,
That *hubris*, the Devil's dastardly work,
Had tempted him toward a paltry perk.

Poor Bernardo, this was too much for him,
For he'd fallen from his lectern to sin,
Causing him to ramble and babble
Among the meanest gaggle and rabble.
Thus, he was confined to his cell and bed
Where he was allowed only water and bread,
Still, he worsened; nothing had changed,
Dropping into a deep depression…deranged.

Ultimately, Levi was called-in to fix
The blue monk with one of his herbal tricks,
La Muerte showed up at the monk's footboard,
Meaning the monk wasn't wanted by the Lord.
Daily, Levi prepared the monk some anise tea
To calm him down and give serenity,
Then Levi explained, "the Lord's greater view
Is to judge us by the work that we do,
For hell would be a pretty crowded lot,

If folks were confined for what they thought.
One of the best traits of our Lord God
Is that He takes a posture of wink and nod."
Praise La Muerte! She'd coached Levi so well,
He even helped the monk going through hell,
Who soon returned to his mendicant work,
Translating tomes of lore without a perk.

Hmm. Levi got to thinking he was top dog,
Because he was riding so high on the hog,

And so, he got cocky and arrogant,
Ascribing to himself the power of cant.
Recall that Levi had a rich neighbor,
From whom he stole hens rather than labor.
It seems Don Rico took a turn for the worse,
Claiming a *brujo* had placed a crass curse
On his soul, causing him to cavort
In brothels and bars to cut his life short,
So without hesitation or demur,
He called on Levi Leyba to do a cure.

Levi never liked this Don Rico guy,
By now, you should know the reason why.
At first, Levi dallied, then he showed up
To find Don Rico's family all pumped-up,
They weren't ready to mourn or to cry,
For Don Rico was ready and willing to buy,
To try to bribe away his mortal jam,
By using his treasured jewels, gems, or ham,
Sheep, pigs, cows, hens, he had plenty of
To bribe mere men but not the Lord above.
(You know Don Rico was without shame,
That's how he'd achieved fortune and fame,

42

To him, the end always justified the means
Which was how he achieved his fiscal schemes.)

At first, he faked a dry, retching whine,
Offering Levi gems, gold, and wine,
But, La Muerte had appeared at the headboard,
Meaning Don Rico was wanted by the Lord,
Signaling Levi on just how to act,
So he recited as a matter of fact:
"I'm sorry, but the Lord is calling you,
And there's nothing anyone can do."

"¡Qué va!" Don Rico shrieked, "this can't be,
What will become of my family?"
Then, he broke into copious crying,
Moaning and groaning, sighing about dying,

Knowing full well that Levi was a sucker,
Who'd pity the mangiest mucker.
Just then, Don Rico hit Levi's weak spot
By offering chickens for his pot,
Levi would have a chicken every day,
To last as long as it would take to pay
For the cure to keep Don Rico alive—
Alas, Levi was tempted by the poultry jive.

La Muerte protested. She was persisting,
Standing at the high headboard, insisting
That Levi should just let things be,
According to the Lord and the Holy See,
She waved both arms, meaning Levi should halt,
God knows, Don Rico's passing was not his fault.
She tried everything to make Levi stop,
Even danced a jig and a bunny-hop,

Making a fool out of herself and the Lord
To prevent Levi from acting untoward.
Pero, que relajé, Levi was too weak,
And Josie, God rest her soul, was too meek,
Therefore, with a cure, Levi went ahead,
Saving Don Rico from the deathbed.

Time passed. Josie and Levi were eating well,
And as far as anybody could tell,
Nothing had come from breaking God's rules,
Which, of course, is the code of fools.
La Muerte was soon at Levi's door
With a heavy heart, bad news, and much more.
Once again, they gathered at the table,
The seats now covered with ermine and sable,

For Josie and Levi were no longer poor
With chickens to eat forevermore.
La Muerte placed two candles on the table top,
One was tall, and the other was not,
She lit both with a flame as white as chalk,
And then she softly shaped her solemn talk:

"I won't be able to say this in one breath,
But, with Don Rico's cure, you didn't cheat death,
Although you used your curative tools
To bend and break one of the Lord's basic rules.
When it's a person's time to go, no one
Can cheat the Lord by making an end-run."
(At this point, our weary Angel of Death
Sighed a tired, aggravated breath.)

"When an end run's done, you should know,
A substitute soul is taken in tow,

For the Lord keeps an exact account
Of the living and the dead, and no amount
Of smoke and mirrors can change His plan,
No matter how hard you try, as try can.
Levi, I hate to break the news this way,
You'll not eat at the table today."

Moan and mope, it was Levi's turn to groan,
You'd a thought he was Don Rico's clone,
The way he moaned, whining and sighing,
Emulating the rich man's crying,
Thinking he was above the Lord's rules,
The ruse, the *viejos* say, of fools.

He pleaded with La Muerte for his life
Claiming no one would care for Josie, his wife.
To no avail, La Muerte was a cold fish,
Though she had once eaten from Levi's dish,
For when the Lord has called and selected you,
There's nothing that anyone can do,
When it comes down to balancing His books,
Our Lord has no favorites, kings, queens, or rooks.

Again, our weary Angel of Death
Sighed a tired, aggravated breath,
Pointing to the candles, one quite small,
The other hardly tall at all:

"Your life was once like the candle that's tall,
With a lengthy wick to burn before you'd fall,
When you disobeyed, by making Rico's cure,
You switched the two life-candles, to be sure.
The short one that is now burning dim
Is your life, though meant to be for him.

Good friend, I am not one prone to cry,
For you had everything money can buy,
Yet, your foolish foibles almost drew a tear,
From me, the righteous have nothing to fear,
And besides giving the Lord the dickens,
You actually sold your life for chickens."
Then, the shortest candle's flame expired,
Levi Leyba's leveraged life retired,
Put to rest, leaving Josie to grow old
With plenty of chickens, so the story's told.

Lawrence: Your tale was delightful,
Can you tell another,
Your bag's so full?

Lupe: ¡*Órale*! Yes, I can. I will be more than glad
To tell you a *chiste* told to me by my Dad.
A chiste mejicano will be a good change,
A tall-tale or joke with a very broad range
Of themes and schemes of human foibles,
Such as, "he who ruins the most gets the spoils."
The *chiste* I'll relate is well known in some parts,
Of an angel and two lovers with fickle hearts.
For a refrain I'll use the Spanish couplet:
Yo soy un Angel de Dios
Y vengo por uno de los dos.
In English it goes:
I am an Angel of God
And, I come for either of you.
In the Spanish language it scans and has a rime,
In English it falls flat, but I guess that's no crime.

Chiste **of the Gentle Angel**

Es qúe, the Lord was unhappy with one Angel,
Who was causing Him much trouble and travail,

And He presumed His Angels obeyed Him better
When He bewailed, cajoled and tightened the fetter.
So he beckoned the gentle angel *Placido.*

Lord: "¡*O-yeh, Placido, ven 'aca, perezoso*!
See here! We manage heaven just like We play cards,
Face up! With all cards on the table, no canards!
We must say, there's no way to be happy today
With your procurement of souls who've passed away."

Placido: "I tell you Boss, I'm not *flojo* or lazy,
But, this *La Muerte* job drives me crazy,
Lord, this job's hard. I liked my job as a guard,
This new job makes me feel like a horse's petard,
Because when I go to earth, I feel like the skunks,
Better to be guarding widows, *niños*, and drunks."

Lord: "To you, being liked by people is important,
You'll find they are not so hot in deportment,
When We sent Our son, they nailed Him to a cross,
Because We kicked them from Eden to show who was
Boss."

Placido: "Boss, that was a long, long time ago,
And still *la gente* are never ready to go,
When people sense I'm in town, they're not at ease,
They avoid *La Muerte* like pestilence and disease.
You've no idea of the image she projects

Of a wanton, weird witch everybody rejects,
I mean *La Muerte,* the Angel of Death, no less,
Always eager to take your soul without regress.
To *la gente,* she's a skeleton carved from wood
Bedecked with purple vestment and a monkish hood,
Her eyes and nose are but hollowed holes in her skull
Whose sinister grin turns *la gente* dull and null.
She slays her victims while they're awake, or in bed,
Taking stringy hanks of hair to hang from her head,
She rides a *carreta,* a rickety chariot,
Armed with bow and arrow to serve as lariat.

La gente's cuentos have it, when it's your time to go,
La Muerte hunts you down with her bow and arrow,
She pierces your heart with the arrow and you die,
Then, she pulls your soul with it to 'Our Sweet-Bye-n-Bye.'

Lord: "We are aware of the dispositions you face,
But We are in the throes of a desperate race,
The pace of births exceeds the rate of passed-on souls,
If left alone, this will cause wars and other woes.
> *Mande con un voz grande:*
> *Yo soy un Angel de Dios*
> *Y vengo por uno de los dos.*

Placido: "*Por Dios,* face it, my spirit isn't in it,
I'd go back to being a guard in a minute!"
The Lord reckoned the chances were slightly slim
To reform the guardian Angel who'd lost his vim.
High blood pressure tactics would do little good,
The Lord lowered His voice to show He understood.

Lord: "Maybe you're going about it the wrong way,

You should tell them: 'Hey you! I am here on His say!'
Don't let them give you a hard time or be sassy,
They like living and don't want to leave the chassis.
Don't take just anybody's Uncle Herman,
Look around, you'll find plenty of vermin.
Take-out any drug pushers you can find,
Without showing pity or mercy of any kind,
Don't take any professors if they whine or yelp,
They already make their own hell without Our help.

Look for Bull riders, or someone with a death wish,
Or, scam artists who bilk widows and the foolish,
Or, politicians who give tax breaks to the rich,
Or, a fickle twosome too vain to keep their hitch.
Pay little mind to what these people have to say,
When it's their turn to go, they'd rather stay.

> *Mande con un voz grande*:
> *Yo soy un Angel de Dios*
> *Y vengo por uno de los dos.*

The Lord's lucid, pep-talk pumped up Placido,
And now he was ready and raring to go.

Placido: "I see now, for people it's never a good time
To give up the Ghost, *que va,* do they ever whine,
I must use a more *macho* assertive approach,
And just show them I won't take '*no*' for a reproach."

Lord: "Atta boy! Atta boy! *Bueno suerte* and bless you,
You'll feel much better once you've brought back a few,
The righteous will thank you, with nothing to fear,

And all the rest? Well, let them cry a salty tear."
Placido commenced to listen to *la gente* talk,
Hovering over their homes like a chicken hawk,
Noting *la gente* was pretty free with their speech,
Making terrible threats and pious pledges to breach.
He hoped to find old derelicts and drunks,
But soon discovered them to be spunky grumps,
Well guarded by the Angel's former peers,
Who shooed him away *con* epithets and jeers.

Next, he flew to a retirement home to try,
Assuming the old folks there were waiting to die,
But, he discovered to his chagrin and surprise,
No one—*ninguno*—was waiting for their demise,
He knew time was wasting when he heard a *viejo* say:
"You bet I'm old! But, I get better every day,
I'm going to live so long, I'll make young girls sigh,
They'll be asking: when's that old fart going to die?"

Waiting for old folks to die was a waste of time,
With advancing age, they get better like old wine,
So he sought out young people to hear what they'd say
Thinking to catch them off guard in their petty play.
At a hotel, he found two lovers in repartee,
Oblivious of what the other had to say:
He says, "My love is greater than yours, this is why,
I have more love for you than are stars in the sky."
She says, "My love is greater, an endless fountain
That flows with the purest water from the mountain."

Our Guardian Angel turned Death was about to leave
When he heard more than a word to give him reprieve,

Thinking, "maybe this is their foolish death-wish?"
And so he flew near to hear more of their gibberish.

He says, "I love you so much, this is surely so,
ThatIwishtobefirsttogo, e-nee-me-nee-my-nee-mow."
She says, "I love you so much, this is certainly true,
I cross my heart and hope to die before you do."

Swoosh! Placido dived down to their front door!
"Knock! Knock!" The lover's heard, "Knock! Knock!"
They heard once more.
He says, "Who's that come rapping at our chamber
door?"
She says, "Yes! Yes! Tell us, tell us forevermore!"

> Yo soy un Angel de Dios
> Y vengo por uno de los dos.

"Hel~lo~o~o! We no~o speak~o mex~e~can~o!"
They both beefed in unison, lying through their teeth.

He was no *stupido,* he knew he'd be tested
By this fickle twosome whose love he'd arrested:
"You shouldn't try to fool me, I've been well coached,
I've come on His say, and I'll not be broached,
Before you go, you should know I'm multilingual,
And can *sprechen parlez-vous con* any gringo,
So I'm telling you two, I'm here for one of you,
Doesn't matter to me, either one of you will do."

Silence and more silence is all he could discern
From the two lovers who knew it was their turn,

> Yo soy un Angel de dios
> Y vengo por uno de los dos.

Still silence prevailed from within the chamber doors,
Not a word was heard from either of the paramours.

"I'll keep a'knocking until you let me in,
Now that's the way it is and always has been!"

Within there still was a silence *muy tremendo,*
They'd gone from crescendo to diminuendo,
Then both chortled concurrently, they chortled fine:
"My dearest darling, would you get the door this time?"

Tom: Ha! It's still the same old story,
A fight for love and glory,
A case of do or die,
Until it's your time to go,
And then—it's put the brakes, whoa!

T. Osprey: Say, feel for the poor Angel of Death?
His job is to come here and steal your breath.
How'd you'd like to get up every blessed day
With the message, you're taking people away
From the only existence they know?
Being a messenger of death would grow
Depressing and tiring, to say the least,
No one would invite you over to feast.

Lolo: Well, someone's got to do the dirty job,
That's why He has His holy Angels to trod.
He lords it over all of them, all right,
They're all slaves, now, they lost the noble fight
To free themselves from the bondage of the Lord,
It's a very old story. You're all bored.

Virgil: *Au contraire*! You've hit it on the head,
    Freedom to the Angels is pretty dead.

Battle of the Angels

In *Paradise Lost*, John Milton told it all,
How Lucifer—Satan—put out the call
For an audience with God to discuss
Equal rights, and to preclude a big fuzz,
Satan asked to sit beside God on His throne,
To reign equally in His heavenly home.
Of course, God wouldn't consent to confer
With anybody, much less Lucifer,
Muttering, "it's a throne he wants, that's swell,
He can man a throne in the chaos of Hell,

Where I'll send other worms and vermin
For Satan and crew to lord over 'em."
To be sure, Satan didn't like God's terms,
To lord over human vermin and worms.
Satan formed an army of massive size
With Beelzebub, the lord of the flies.
They rigged cannons on chariots to fire
Hundreds of iron balls that made a mire
Of the Lord's pearly gates and flower gardens,
Taking no prisoners! Granting no pardons!

Gabriel led other Angels to strike back,
According to Milton, in counter-attack,
By lifting Heaven's hills, like a quilt,
And covering Satan's troops with dirt and silt,
Entombing them under debris foot-to-face,
Taking them a long time to dig from that place.

Of the many things eternal life grants
Is the time to dig-out dirt without recants,
And Satan's troops did, tossing the debris back
In a hailing rock and dirt counterattack,
Followed by Satan's cannons blazing away,
Blasting holes through anything in the way.

The Lord's army of angels fought back hard,
Still Satan advanced to the Lord's front yard,
Nightfall came, and Satan's army rested,
Surmising the good angels had been bested,
But, the Lord wouldn't allow. He sent His Son,
Ordering: "Don't come back till the war's won!"
To shove Satan from His Father's home,
Jesus determined to go it alone,
Setting the standard for other princes,
Who sought to free kingdoms from deadly cinches.
(The brave Beowolf learned from Jesus the Son,
Wrestling Grendel with help from no one,
Sparing his men from battle in harm's way,
For sons of kings, that's what the sagas say.)

Jesus sat atop His chariot-throne,
Beneath it, four cherubs carried its dome,
Each cherub was wound-round to form an eye,
Affixed to carry the throne through the sky.
Off they thrust toward the tumultuous hills,
Blasting and belching billowing trills
Of sparks and flickering flames burning wild,
Pricking perdition without mercy-mild.
In the hills, He found Satan's army resting,
And decided to attack without testing
His devised weapon of mass destruction
That spit furious fire on His instruction:

Ten thousand thunderbolts
thrust from His right hand!
Splattering fire and plague over the land!
The lightning fires were easy to subside,
The plague was too deadly to abide.
Satan and army were forced to retreat,
The germ warfare had them thoroughly beat,
Not a pleasant smell, nor a pretty sight,
Leaving it to poet Dante to cite
The anguish and misery that befell
The fallen angels who drank from Satan's well.

Buster: Truth be known, try as hard as I can,
Boy howdy, I'm no big John Milton fan.
Said he wrote *Paradise Lost* to make plain
The arcane pain of Christian reign,
To justify the ways of God to man,
To explain Christianity best he can.
But, I flat-out missed getting its grand theme
What with the epic's complex scheme,
And its classical sidetracks,
Hobbled tight with convoluted syntax.

Lawrence: Let's go back to Lupe's tale about work,
I wouldn't call Placido a lazy jerk.
In fact, a good job should keep you happy,
Giving you a genuine reason to be.

It's been a fact since antiquity,
The only reason to have slavery
Is to force someone to do the hard work,
No, I can't call Placido a lazy jerk.

Virgil: Religious sanctions made people behave,
Even accept the status of a slave.
Since it was the will of God you had to work,
Could be the most boring job, without a perk,
You worked in servitude for later on,
And your reward came in the Great Beyond.

Tom: Don't like hard work, won't bray or brag,
Hard work is nothing but a drag,
In olden days, workers would sing a song,
In rhythm to their work, they'd sing along.

Lolo: What's with the heavy metal jazz?
Good tales should have some pizzaz.
Wait till you hear about Mrs. Brady
And her Chihuahua pooch named *Lady*.

4

TOMMY SPINS SENTIMENT INTO SONG

Tommy proves to be a true troubadour,
Singing songs he'd composed before,
He first sings a make-up-words kind of song
For everyone to enjoy and sing along.
Then Lupe tells of Manuel who digs for coal,
To dig soldiers from sand becomes his goal,
Last, Tom turns to a happy, carefree song,
Not a makeup-words-as-you-go-along song.

Bob: I do believe the next person to go
Should be Tommy *the* Tornado,
He's the leader of a big, ole band
Known as '*The Fireballs*' in the land.
Tom really digs and plays the blues and soul,
Also sings some country and rock 'n roll,
His songs are used in movies like *Forrest Gump*,
Showing he's no one-trick pony in a slump.
He now teaches the sociology
Of working class musicology,
And so now, without further adieu,
Here's Tommy Tornado to entertain you.

Tom: Hey man, it feels good, it feels great,
To be on the professor's slate!
You know, we had our day on stage
When Fireball hits were the rage:
Fireball hit the charts in '59,
And that was for the very first time.
Next was first pick with *Torquay*

By the disc jockeys in L.A.,
Then, *Bulldog* showed our tunes could grow,
Even got us on the Dick Clark Show.

So what the hay? We didn't care,
We were making magic in the air.
Then, *Sugar Shack* hit Number One,
We were on a roll, having fun,
Top of the charts, five weeks in a row,
For small town boys, that's a good show,
That ditty took us pretty far, Listen up,
I'll sing you a bar:
"There's a crazy little shack
    beyond the tracks,
And everybody calls it the Sugar Shack."

Bob: "Fireballs" is a tough-enough rocking name,
Weren't you the first band of fire-folk fame?

Tom: Yeah, it all began at the Raton High gym,
We entered a show, playing and praying to win,
The M.C. didn't have a clue what to call us
Till we jammed out a tune by Jerry Lee Lewis,
It was the only song we knew for encore,
And the kids were stomping and shouting,
"More! More! More!"
                —Tom Sings—
"You shake my nerves an' you rattle my brains,
Your kind of lovin' drives a man insane, Goodness gra-
cious, Great Balls of Fire!"

Great Balls of Fire whipped up a hellacious flame,
The kids stomping in rhythm, shouting our name:

"Fi-re Balls! Fi-re Balls!" They yelled good and loud,
And we got a flamin' name from that cool crowd.

Bob: With you, humility was a true trait,
Get on with your story, we can hardly wait.

Tom: Hey-y-y, man
Stop the van
To git my guitar
'Fore we go too far.

Bob: Well-el-el, I dunno?
Gotta long way to go.

All: Boo, hiss, and all,
Stop the van, man!
Or, Tom'll bawl.

Bob: I pulled the van beside the road
        To avoid the professor's goad.

Tom: Be back in a jiff,
        'Fore I cause a tiff.

Bob: With that, Tommie jumped out,
Untied his guitar and came about,
Returning with guitar and pick,
We hit the road at a steady lick.
Tom tuned his acoustic guitar
Before we'd traveled very far,
Then launched into his riding song,
A *makeup-the-words-as-you-go-along* song.

Cowboy Riding Song

        —All sing along & Tom strums guitar—
O-o-oh!
Do you want to do what cowboys do,
All day and night?
They dog a bull, they're always cool,
That's what cowboys do.

Now, preachers preach, teachers teach,
But cowboys ri-i-ide.
And, bakers bake, cakers cake,
But cowboys ri-i-ide.
O-o-h!
Do you want to do what cowboys do,
All day and night?
They rope a cow, they never bow,
That's what cowboys do.

Now, plumbers plum, hummers hum,
But cowboys ri-i-ide,
And miners mine, whiners whine
But cowboys ri-i-ide.

O-o-oh!
Do you want to do what cowboys do,
All day and night?
They skin a mule, they're always blue,
That's what cowboys do.

Now, liners line, diners dine,
But cowboys ri-i-ide,
And, piners pine, signers sign,

But cowboys ri-i-ide.

O-o-oh!
Do you want to do what cowboys do,
All day and night?
Do your best, fill in the rest,
That's what cowboys do!
—Singing Fades—

Tom: Sure like the words to this little ditty,
I made them up, down in O.K. City,
You can ride forever with this type song,
Just make up the words as you go along.

Inger: Some say, you can tell men from boys
By comparing the price of their toys,
And, I say that you can't go wrong,
If you judge boys by their song.

Bob: I'm not sure I know what you mean,
    But you're fitting into the scheme.

Osprey: Like a fresh tossed salad,
    That was one crispy ballad.

Buster: Boy howdy, don't wanna split hairs,
But if anybody here cares
For cowboy ballads, well, Tom's
Make-up-words-as-you-go-along song
Isn't strictly a cowboy ballad,
Shoot, that's no matter—it's still valid.

Lolo: I agree. It's not a cowboy ballad,
Yet, there's more than one way to make a salad,

For Tom's song is good in-of-itself
And shouldn't be tossed off the shelf.

Bob: Lupe, amigo,
Toss up your folkloric salad
And sing us a Latino ballad.

Lupe: *Ah sí,* I will. I will discuss
The workings of a ballad of this type,
It's one of the oldest types known to us,
Called the *corrido,* the '*run,*' if you like.
Corridos generally tell somber tales,
Heroes, heroines with their illusions,
In a futile quest that often fails
To do justice and other delusions.
The first stanza presents a precise display
Of the ballad's plot, or it gives a straight
Forward description of all those who play
The fortuitous odds against their fate.
All remaining stanzas are events
Strung into chronological order,
The episodes told in timely sequence,
By a first-rate historical recorder.
When all the pertinent events are told,
And the saga's no other place to go,
The balladeer declares flat-out cold:
"This is the end of my corrido."
Good troubadours shriek a stridulous trill
To a toe-tapping rhythm, and they'll go
To any length to give the girls a thrill,
¡*Yé-yé-yé-yé!* Trilling in tremolo.
Since I'm in no way Tommy Tornado,
And certainly can't go the singing route,
Consider my corrido to be so-so,

A lame imitation as I drone it out,
So here's my corrido as sung to me,
Of a man's quest for simple dignity.

El Corrido de Manuel Ribera

This true tale is highly mentioned
By miners and troops now pensioned,
Of *Manuelito Ribera*,
Born before *la primavera*.

As a boy, he played free
In the hills of the *piñón* tree,
And he ran free with the deer
While the antelope foraged near.

He left school, his father was ill,
To work the mines, a bitter pill,
Where work was to shovel and pick,
And don't give Bossman surly lip.

Working the coal was mighty grim,
The gape of life and death was slim,
The air was gassy, lights were dim,
Manuel asked God to care for him.

The roof caved-in, good men died,
Gas pocket blew, more widows cried,
The men organized to save their hide,
Bossman fired them—union denied.

To Manuel, this was very wrong,
Miners have rights to work along,

He led a picket in the dawn,
To form a union, they were strong.

They got their demands, which were few,
On Manuel, Boss turned the screw
With the Draft Board as his tool,
He drafted Manuel into World War II.

Aíí, yí-yí, Manuelito worked to make us free,
Aíí, yí-yí, Manuelito fought to keep us free.

Plunged into war when he crossed the sea,
Battle of the Bulge—the infantry.

They fought tough and hard as can be
To deny the Germans a victory.

Suddenly, they were pushed under
By a rain of cannon thunder,
Men were falling, dying asunder,
That Manuel lived was a wonder.

The men pinned down by spewing lead,
Trying to move would make them dead,
Then a big bomb dropped in their stead,
Burying five men toe to head.

Manuel ran fast with his shovel
To dig the men from the hovel,
He lunged through the hellish rubble,
When shot, he crawled through the stubble.

He dug with the shovel in hand,
To free the men was his command,

"Crawl from here!" he charged in remand,
As each soldier crawled from the sand.

Manuel began to crawl away,
Knowing five men lived one more day,
The bullets continued to spray, Three bullets pierced
his back, And, still he lay....

This ends the corrido as it was sung to me,
Of Manuel Ribera who fought to make us free,
Manuelito now rests in the *camposanto*,
En el nombre del Padre, del Hijo, y Espíritu Santo.

Bob: Still...Silent. All of us were still,
None of us could speak, we'd lost our will
To utter a crass comment or wise crack,
Lupe's ballad had thrown us off track,
Our tongues tied tautly with emotions,
Of rage and respect for Manuel's devotions

To the bloody fights for human rights for all,
And his ready willingness to heed the call.
For a very long ten minutes we sat still
While the van floated on the surreal,
Finally, Tom who wears his heart on his sleeve,
Spoke up, breaking the silence, making reprieve.

Tom: Hey, man, that story bummed me out,
Your Bossman needs a good punch in the snout,
The way the Bossman treated Manuelito,
I'm ashamed to call myself a gringo.

Smokey: With Manuel, I would be proud to muster,
He was an original mold buster.

Lupe: Manuel was cut from a rugged mold,
Like others whose stories haven't been told,
Mejicano soldiers are known for their bravery
And have been cited for their gallantry.
They fought in every war for the U.S. of A.,
Their courage, their heroism never did sway,
Many of these men died in the heat of battle,
Buster would say, they died with boots in the saddle.
Their names and deeds are displayed in the Pentagon,
Here's a tribute by President Lyndon Johnson:
"The soldiers of Mexican origin fought courageously,
They gave their lives, when need be, valiantly."
Congressional Medals of Honor they have got,
An early grave, for many of them, was their lot.
In the year 2,000, thirty-six was their count,
As times passes, their numbers will mount.

Ay, qué lástima. I learned of these gentle men
From Raul Morin, a soldier who took the pen
To tell their tales for the red, white and blue,
Of courageous and intrepid deeds, all too true.
Among the Valiant was the name of his book,
I read it long ago; it's worth a second look.

Inger: That these boys died is very sad,
That war happens is very bad,

On this theme, I'll have more to say
When the turn to tell comes my way.

Tom: Man, this stuff is heavy!
You've laid on a levy
On our cheery bevy.
Since we don't have any beer,
I'm gonna bring some cheer,
So listen up to this tune
    I been toying with,
I took it from an Indian myth
That can be told, or sung aloud,
So I'll sing it, since that's allowed.

Fly ~ Fly ~ Away

They say
The breeze is beautiful,
But no one I know
Can hold her still,
Don't cage her in,
Don't clip her wings,
Let her go
To have her flings,
Yes ~ let her
fly ~ fly ~ away.

They say
The breeze is wonderful,
But no one I know
Can hold her still,
Don't fence her in,
Don't hold her tight,
Let her go
To take her flight,
Yes ~ let her
fly ~ fly ~ away.

So come and fly
The sky with me,

For no one I know
Should be more free,
Won't cage you in,
Just let you be,
Won't clip your wings
So you'll be free,
To fly ~ fly away,
fly ~fly ~ away....

Smokey: In wind, rain, fire and sky,
If you love her, you must let her fly.

Inger: Tom, in your songs I saw two type-men,
The first type should take up the pen
To compose a male chauvinistic creed,
As a holdover from some dying breed
Of Jurassic cowboys who can't change,
Riding alone over their home on the range.
But, if your second type carries out his belief,
He'll be regarded with some relief
By all the gals under the sun,
After all, most gals just want to have fun.

Buster: I think Inger's wrong
To come off so almighty strong
About Tom's *Cowboy Riding Song*,
It's 'bout freedom to move on,
Like Tom's tender second song
Where the heroine's no hop-a-long.

Virgil: One positive factor I see
Is that neither steals its melody
From other folk or classic compositions,
Which happened to rock-an-roll by the tons.

Inger: Ho! Good ol' boy boosters,
Or, more like cocky roosters,
Perching on the corral fence
And crowing in Tom's defense.
Last time I checked the critic's folder,
Art was still in the eye of the beholder.

Bob: Whoa! We're getting vitriolic and uptight,
Let's agree. Tom's singing turned out all right,
And plaudits and kudos to Lupe, too,
For reciting his heartfelt corrido.
Now, let's try to pitch our dialogue civil,
One note above dull, two above drivel.

Lupe: *Verdad.* We should try to tone down,
Picking our words so as not to drown
Each other. Let's use the old dicho:
No hay conversación sin contradicción,
That is: there is no conversation
                without contradiction.

Virgil: Very good. Splendid. Yes, of course
That's the nature of discourse,
We simply agree to disagree
And treat each other civilly,
Recognizing sharp differences may exist,
Recognizing sharp differences may persist,

Yet, for progress we have to insure
We allow free discourse to occur.

Lolo: Right on. That's true in the arts, too,
Each holds tight to a point-of-view,
But we should listen in a civil way
To what others believe and have to say,
You might learn something new
And be better for it, too.

Lawrence: Well, I'm new to the storytelling art
And wonder how to tell art forms apart,
Were Tom's tunes tales at all?
With Lupe's ballad, Manuel took up the call
To fight for rights, but with Tom's songs
There were no conflicts, no rights and wrongs.

Virgil: Ah, it's clear. The difference here
Is between the troubadour and balladeer,

Both songsters were poets in their own right,
Meter and rhyme squeaky-clean tight.
These songsters thrived in the Middle Ages
Just a rank above knightly pages,
The troubadour sang of courtly love
Comparing ladies to birds, sparrow or dove,
As in Tom's courtly tune, *"Fly, Fly Away,"*
A lady likened to a bird in every way.
But it was balladeers sang a story
Of right and wrong, tragedy and glory,
As in Lupe's ballad, Manuel takes the banner
To fight right against wrong in every manner.

Lawrence: Well, yes. Tom's tunes fit into our fest,
Do they count in our tale-telling contest?

Bob: Hmm. We decided some kind of prize would go
To the best tale about folks, high or low,
Or to the best crafted story or scheme
That spieled a splendid, redeeming theme.

Buster: Boy howdy, if we're going by the book,
Seems to me Tom's still got a hook
In the line "best crafted story *or* scheme
That spieled a splendid, redeeming theme."

Bob: With Buster's point, everybody agreed
To move on, to concede
Tom's tunes required respect
For their theme and over-all affect.

5

LAWRENCE LECTURES ON

TORTS & RETORTS

A tad of a lad grows hair on his hand,
Causing Joe Jones to take Doc to the stand,
Baa Baa Bailey, a lazy lawyer as such,
Uses the insanity plea too much,
Youngster Abel turns into a rocket
By sticking a butter knife in a socket,
And Judge Sancho disposes of dirt-ball sleaze,
Greedy, grubby liars who deceive with ease.

Bob: How best to introduce Lawrence Carrow,
A learned man to the marrow,
Who earned a *Juris Doctorate* from Stanford,
And a Ph.D. in ethics from Oxford.
Without the benefit of a silver spoon,
He was born in the back of a saloon,
Not much more than a wooden shack
That rattled as the train passed on the track,
His mother sold liquor and tended bar,
While his father cooked on a Pullman car.

Growing up, he met men of all kinds,
Those who worked with their backs, or minds,
The candid, honest men worked with their backs,
Although in other virtues, there were lacks.
He learned from men who wore the tailored suits
That knowledge was basic to their pursuits,

Just where did I get all this poor-boy stuff?
I read Larry's bio, that's no bluff,
It's posted on the campus WEB site,
Accessible to you both day and night.
He tells of tough times in younger years,
Helping his mother tend bar and sell beers,
Larry, tell me, did I depict you well,
Or are there other details I should tell?

Lawrence: Bob, in general, you did a swell job,
After Virgil's intro your heart must throb,
I thought for sure by now you'd be downright curt,
You weren't and I've no reason to be hurt.
All the tales I tell along the way
Are based on what my mother would say:
"They say that talk is cheap,
That little does it reap,
So what does it matter
If we chit-chat and chatter?"

The Hairy Hand Case

The case I can't erase from law school days
Is the one we called the *"Hairy Hand Case."*
One day Joe Jones was working in his yard
With his son Jimmie, who was working hard,
Jim was cutting wood with a table saw,
When in went his hand, the palm of his paw,
Right in the saw! Blood went a-splurgin'!
Jones rushed Jimmie to the neighbor surgeon,
Who rushed him, and none too soon,
To the hospital emergency room.

The bleeding was stopped with twenty stitches,
And the hand was fixed with several hitches:
No nerves were cut, but it would be a while
Before he could splay his hand in style,
It would be stiff, and then loosen up,
Wouldn't be long he could lift a cup.
Another hitch, a large unsightly scar,
Crossing, bisecting the palm pretty far.

"Please Dr. Casey, fix Jim's hand," begged Jones,
"You're the best with wounds and broken bones,
For you, fixing a scar would be a cinch,
Bet you could in a pinch of an inch."
"Well," Casey replied, "I guess I could try
To smooth the palm of this game little guy,
Because a plastic surgeon I'm not,
There'll be no fee to fix the tender tot."
So, then, the date for surgery was set,
And Jim was wheeled into a room and prepped,
Skin from the arm was grafted to the palm,
Jim, through it all, was very calm,
The scar was gone, and he went back to school,
With two good palms to learn the Golden Rule.

Three years later, the hand began to sprout
A hairy crop, causing Jim to pout,
Pals, I don't like to sound crass and mean,
But such a hairy palm you've never seen!
"Well, to heck with a hairy hand!" cried Jones,
Wasn't long he was on the telephones,
Where he found a lawyer most eager
To make bucks like a National Leaguer.
In our legal system, anyone can sue,
Whether the alleged grievance is false or true,

So Jones took the good doctor to court,
Suing Doc Casey for a wrongful tort
Against his young son who suffered so great,
Have you seen a dark, hairy hand of late?
(It seems the boy would go to any means
To avoid using hair-removing creams.)
Now, this is no different as a tort suit,
You see, Jones was out after Doc's loot,
And like most cases of liability,
There was no pretense at civility,
Jones charged this was a plain case of negligence,
That Doc had performed beyond his competence.
Casey retorted, making a defense,
At plastic surgery he made no pretense:

"Why, Jim's father begged me to fix the cut,
Although I sent no charges to his hut.
The reason I fixed the palm without a fee
Is because I don't do plastic surgery.
As I had pledged, I got rid of the scar,
The boy seemed pleased and happier, by far."
The judge was madder than the Mad Hatter,
And almost broke his what'cha-call-it bladder,
With little patience, nor room on his docket
For suits seeking the sagging pocket.
With the *Hairy Hand Case* what should it be,
Should Doc be punished or fined a fee?

Tom: What a jive turkey for a son!
A dark, hairy hand would be fun.

Buster: Seems to me Dad's cooking up a big deal,
Making a mountain out of a molehill.

Lawrence: Pals, get real about a solution,
You're not close to a resolution,
Okay, here's what the judge decided
On this case over which he presided:
Joe Jones would provide his son a razor,
Hand-held, electric, or chargeable laser,
To shave daily that hairy, handsome crop
From Jimmy's palm in a close-cut lop.
And, Doc Casey would desist from the mystique
Of doing surgery that was plastíque.
The lawyer? Well, the judge broke his bubble,
He got nothing for all of his trouble,
If he should bring trivial suits again,
The judge would give him to our plastic surgeon,
Whom you'd remember, if you'd retrace,
You'd never ask Casey to work your face.

Virgil: What the world needs now
Are honest lawyers true to their creed,
Whether defending for gold or a sow,
Lawyers should be honest in word and deed.

Lawrence: Honest lawyers are not that hard to find,
So long as they keep this old proverb in mind:
"Be cautious with your boast,
Chickens come home to roast."
The proverb shows up in several tales
Recorded in Londonderry and Wales.

Baa Baa Bailey, Esq.

Baa Baa Bailey was the lawyer's nickname,
And indolence was the name of his game,
For he hardly took any cases to fight

To defend a client and do what's right.
On occasion, when he did assume a case,
He'd ply a defense, which was lame and base,
That his curried clients were nuts all along
And couldn't discern to tell right from wrong.

He never lost a case, he would brag and boast,
Forgetting that chickens come home to roast.
His tried and true cases were so few
That his bills were perennially overdue,
Causing his wife to complain all the time:
"What with all the duplicity and crime,
You should have many frivolous cases
To build a solid, monetary bases,
But, no, you hardly ever go to court,
And hardly ever have cash to report."

Grumble and gripe, that's all wife Kate did,
Until Baa Baa tired and blew his lid,
"Gall durn! What will it take for you to forsake?
To cease and desist? To quit the quake?"
Right off, Kate said it would suffice,
"If you got me a new dress, pretty and nice,
And so the tailor can design it fast,
Here! Bring him my mannequin last."

Baa Baa took the last to the tailor in town,
Known for his quick work with down and gown,
Who soon finished the dress for Kate to wear,
Suitable for galas and the County Fair.
Promising to pay by the end of day,
Baa Baa took it to his wife straight away.
Baa Baa acted in his usual way,
Never intending to make good to pay,

Instead, he coached Kate on what to do
When the tailor came to collect his due:
"Just say, I'm crazy and gone over deep,
Fantasizing that I'm a bleating sheep,
When the trusting tailor asks to get paid,
I'll subject him to a babbling charade,
Blathering and blurting out something funny,
Instead of giving him any money."
The next day, the tailor came for his dough,
Unaware of Baa Baa's devious m.o.
Kate played her part to a tee,
Knowing Baa Baa didn't have the tailor's fee.
She met the naïve tailor at the door
To feed him a pack of lies, nothing more,
About how Baa Baa fell off the deep-end,
And was so crazy, he'd no mind to mend,
To make good on the tailor's fee
Was not possible, due to his insanity.

Just then, Baa Baa showed up, walking on all fours,
Baaing and babbling as he paced the floors,
"Baa, baa! Baa, baa! And so forth and so on,
"Baa, Baa! Baa, Baa! And so forth and so on."
After all of that, Kate still had the gall
To ask the tailor to adjust the dress's fall,
(He refused as a way of saving face,
Expecting pay for work is no disgrace.)

Baa Baa's charade worked on the trusting tailor,
Who went away, feeling a failure,

Knowing he'd been fleeced by a crafty fox,
Who'd bilked him of bucks for bagel and lox,
For how could you charge a lawyer so sly,

Or milk a curdled cow that had gone dry?
Thereby, did Baa Baa's reputation spread,
How he'd used craziness to make his bread.

Wasn't long a gambler heard about the hoax
As the word about it spread among the folks,
So he went to see Baa Baa straight away,
To represent him for debts he couldn't pay.
Granted, Baa Baa was indolent and lazy,
But he was a far cry from being crazy,
So, at first, he turned down the gambler's plea,
Leaving the gambler stranded up a tree.
The gambler, unable to accept the spurn,
Looked up Kate to discuss his concern,
After all, Baa Baa was the gambler's last hope
To prevent hanging from a creditor's rope.
Whining how Baa Baa could make good money
By playing along and acting funny,
He begged Kate to coax the demurring Baa Baa,
To take the case as a last hurrah.

She did. Yet, Baa Baa did not willingly consent,
Putting up a lame and lukewarm dissent,
She persisted, insisting he take the case,
Working for a living was no disgrace.
Grumble, gripe, and grumble, she would not relent,
Until Baa Baa conceded to repent,
To put on this one last specious pretense,
Using insanity as a defense.

While waiting for the trial day,
Baa Baa coached the gambler on just what to say:
"No matter who asks you a question,
Roll your eyes and pay them no attention,

Make wild gestures, slink in your seat,
Utter sheer nonsense, babble, gabble, and bleat,
Such as, 'Baa, baa! Baa baa! And so forth and so on!
Baa, baa! Baa, baa! And so forth and so on!'

Even when asked to state your full name,
Arch your back, crane your neck, continue to feign,
'Baa, baa! Baa, baa! And so forth and so on,
Baa, baa! Baa, baa! And so forth and so on.'

The jury was selected without much toil,
And the trial began, according to Hoyle,
The lawyer for the plaintiffs started right in,
Making a case against the gambler's sin,
Which was that he was in debt, up to his gills,
For gambling and spending without paying bills.

The plaintiffs produced a lengthy account,
Showing the gambler allowed his bills to mount,
While he continued to spend and buy,
Though at craps, he usually threw snake-eye,
And his luck at cards was equally bad
In casinos from London to Baghdad.
Baa Baa knew he had the upper hand
When the time came for making a stand,
He called the gambler to the witness seat,
Who was dressed dapper, so trim and neat.

Now Baa Baa concisely crafted his terms
To lead the gambler to make absurd returns:
"For the record, good sir, tell us your name?"
"Baa, baa! Baa, baa! And so forth and so on."
"And, what do you make of your creditors' claim?

"Baa, baa! Baa, baa! And so forth and so on."
The jovial judge was jarred with chagrin
And interrupted by jumping right in,
"Say, you're singing off key? What's your tune?"

The gambler: "Baa, baa! Baa, baa! So forth, so on."
The judge exclaimed, "you're crazy as a loon!"
"The defense rests its case," Baa Baa said,
"My client's lost the marbles in his head."

The jury sequestered for a short while
And returned their verdict in prompt style:
"We find for the gambler, because he's not sane,
Making him pay would be crass and profane,
Instead, we think he should be confined for life,
Or until he overcomes his addictive strife."
The plaintiffs' lawyer nodded in disbelief,
For his creditor-clients got no relief,
As for the gambler, he was hauled away
Without making arrangements to pay.

Every weekend Baa Baa took great pain
To visit the asylum for the insane,
Where the gambler was confined to stay,
Playing cards and shooting dice the livelong day.
Every weekend when Baa Baa asked for his fee,
The gambler responded in zestful glee,
"Baa, baa! Baa, baa! And so forth and so on."

That's all the luckless gambler would utter,
Even when Baa Baa brought jelly and butter
To spice up the gambler's spare meal
Of charred chives, endives, and dill.

No matter how much Baa Baa would boast,
His chickens eventually came home to roast.

Inger: Hmmm. Another lawyer's story
Alleging allegory.

Lawrence: Oh, we are a most litigious nation,
Causing an over-pricing situation,
No matter what firms make: knives, forks, or flutes,
They raise their prices to pay for lawsuits.

Of Sockets & Kid Rockets

Let's say Jones buys a set of butter knives,
Priced way too much in the double fives,
He brings them home, puts them on the table
Out of reach from his youngest son, Abel.

Remember Jones' hairy-handed son?
Well, let's say he decides to have some fun
By giving a knife to the younger boy,
Telling Abel the knife's nothing but a toy.
Abel crawls to the wall fast as a rocket
To stick the knife into a live socket,
Wang! The socket thrusts him across the room,
Landing Abel in the sink with a boom.
Abel starts to cry and make a stink,
He's bottom-side up with head in the sink,
Though not hurt, the youngster's had quite a shock
From a knife that wasn't under lock.
Joe Jones sues the Bowie Knife Company
For failure to warn him sufficiently
Of dangers when putting knives in sockets,
Or how knives can turn kids into rockets.

Of course, the Bowie Knife Company knows
They may end up paying through the nose
If they get too tough with litigious Jones,
Not to mention, bad PR and other groans.
It's simpler for them to settle out-of-court
Than stain their image with a charge of tort.
The settlement is cheaper than the headache
Of fighting trumped-up charges for the sake
Of truth and justice, and all the rest of that,
That's not where the bottom line's at.
Fifty-five dollar butter knives may cost more
Next time you go to the cutlery store.

Virgil: In this socket case, it's easy to see
The issue is responsibility,
The fault's in the Jones' older boy,
Who told Abel the knife was but a toy.

Lawrence: Oh, yes, it does come down to that,
Being responsible for the way we act,
If all people were good, we'd need no laws,
Seems we behave best under the lion's paws,

As in tales told in *Don Quijote de la Mancha*,
Spotlighting a loyal page Sancho Panza,
But, I've placed them down in Old Mexico
After I saw a *Cantinflas* show in Calexico.

The Tailor's Tort

There was a legendary Mexican judge
Who heard cases where Angels feared to trudge,
Everyone called him Señor Don Sancho
And never laughed at his Tijuana poncho,

Which he wore over his robe for every case,
I admit it was hard to keep a straight face,
Especially when he wore the ten-gallon hat,
Bending down both ears where the hat sat.
For a judge who didn't look so dignified,
He rendered judgments highly rarefied,
And since his decisions were tight as a trap,
Lawyers rarely gave him grief, lip, or crap.
Because of his knack to cut to the chase,
His trials clipped along at a heady pace
Without bogging down in legal silt,
As in the case when both men shared the guilt:
A tailor brought a jailer to Sancho's court
Over an unpaid bill, the tailor's tort,
Both men were known to be scandalous knaves,
Who behaved as though we still lived in caves.
Say you took cloth to this tailor for a tie,
He'd keep the surplus and conjure a lie,
Saying, "there's little left of your cloth,"
Or that "the surplus was chewed by a moth."
As for the jailer, he was just as greedy,
In winter, he kept the jail cold and seedy,
Knowing no one would stop to inquire
Why it was he didn't build a fire?
Or, what did he do with the money for heat?
Honestly, both knaves could be trusted to cheat.

Judge Sancho convened the trial in court,
"Tell us, tailor, of the import of your tort."
"Señor Don Sancho, I bring you my case
Against this jailer with a *tortuga's* face.

Yesterday, he came into my small shop
With a fine, woolen cloth for me to crop,

He placed the fine cloth in my hands and asks:
'With this wool cloth, can you make me some caps?'
I mentioned I could make some fine caps
That would bring him warmth and plenty of wraps.
'How many? Two? Three?' He kept on asking,
'Up to five,' I replied, without masking.
Now that I made the caps he won't pay me,
Even though I charged him a picayune fee."

"Is this true?" Sancho asked of the jailer,
"Are these the facts as told by the tailor?"

"Yes," replied the jailer, "they're as true as can be,
Now ask to see the caps he made for me."

"Well?" Sancho asked, "did you bring the five caps?
And don't give me any *buts* or *perhaps*.

The tailor tautly tensed up and scoffed,
Wiggling his eyebrows and staring aloft,
"If I hadn't made the caps, I'd not be here,
I'd be at the bar crying in my beer,
Yes, of course, I'll show them; I'm not so dumb,"
Thus, he showed them on his fingertips and thumb,
Sputtering as he held his hand in a splay,
"I made five finger caps; now he should pay."
By now, Sancho wanted to laugh out loud,
But, he didn't want to encourage the crowd
Who would've laughed both knaves out of town,
Instead, he adjusted his hat and gown,
And leaned on his desk hands in his sleeves
While grinning at these epitomes of sleaze.
He proclaimed, "both of you must concede
You're being punished by your tawdry greed,

You, jailer, desire to have many caps,
You, tailor, would gyp the sorriest saps,
I'm ready to give you my final thought
Of this tedious case, which you have brought:

Each of you will lose money in this case,
Say *adios*. Money's gone without trace,
The caps? Jailer lend one to each inmate,
Starting with the one who's least reprobate,
As for you, tailor, you won't get your fee
But are giving back to the community.
This should teach you knaves to cut the gyps,
And some inmates will have warm finger tips."

Smokey: Judge Don Sancho was sagacious and wise,
Was he that way with duplicities and lies?

Lawrence: For Sancho, that case was a piece of cake,
He was wise to the torts most knaves could bake.
His hardest cases dealt with men who lie
With the ease it takes to eat your mother's pie,
There are men so bold they'd fool a polygraph,
Such was this case of the old man and his staff.

Lending Loans to Liars

Two tired elders came to see the judge,
First to speak was the lady muddied with sludge,
Mrs. Ruby Lain was the alleged aggrieved,
Charging that by Eddie Pons she'd been deceived:
"Judge, with heavy heart I come before your stand
To grieve against this man with staff in hand.
Last year, I lent Eddie many a buck,

He was hard-up and down on his luck,
Yesterday, I asked him to pay me back,
He said I'd know better if I'd kept track,
For Ed claims to have paid me once before
And doesn't want to pay me back anymore.
But, as sure as summer leaves in September,
If Ed paid me back, I don't remember."
Then Eddie Pons, with staff in hand, made his stand,
He appeared to have walked on drier land:
"In all my years, I never told a lie,
I wouldn't know how to give it a try,

So how can I make Ruby understand
I once put the money in her hand?
I would swear before God to end this grudge,
If the pledge were ministered by the judge."

Don Sancho asked: "What of this proposition?
Ruby, would it change your disposition
If Eddy with staff in hand were to swear,
Would you consider his pledge to be fair?"
Ruby answered: "if he'd swear on the *Good Book*
That he'd paid me back and was not mistook,
That he'd put the fifty bucks in my hand,
Then, I'll quit this claim I've made at your stand."

Thereupon, Eddie Pons took the stand,
Placing his staff in Ruby's limp hand,
Putting his right palm down on the *Good Book*,
To where everyone could have a good look.
He solemnly swore on the judge's command
That he'd placed the bucks in Ruby Lain's hand:
"As I put my hand on this here *Bible*,

I know the Lord will hold me liable
If I were to lie, prevaricate, or fib,
But, as true as Adam had one less rib,
I know I've placed the bucks in her palm
To placate her pleas and give her calm."
Thereupon, Ruby Lain who now held the staff,
Let out a long sigh and a nervous laugh,
Saying that, "Eddie has a Christian soul,
If he feigns to lie, he'll pay the toll,
I guess I'll never see those bucks,
Lending loans to liars really sucks."

Eddie Pons grabbed the staff from Ruby's hand,
Commencing to leave the stand, beating the band,
Sancho called the departing debtor back,
Stopping him cold as he made hasty track:
"Stop! Come back, you lugubrious lout!
I'm not done with your devious bout!"

The judge retrieved the staff to check it out,
To satisfy and quell his aching doubt,
He sensed Eddie Pons was lying through his gums,
Eddie would send weeds and call them mums.
Sancho noted this was a huge walking stick,
About six feet long and three inches thick,
Seems Eddie Pons applied some kind of bore
To drill the center into a hollow core.
Sancho ran his hand along the stick's side
Till he touched a knothole and caused it to slide,
The knothole slipped, just like a sliding door,
Sancho could peer within the stick's core.
Eddie had stuffed the staff with money,
Making his solemn pledge oddly funny,

Claiming he hadn't distorted or lied,
Ruby had held the staff with the bucks inside.
He claimed he'd told the truth on the stand,
That he'd placed the bucks in Ruby's hand.
Sancho was not swayed by Eddie's trickery,
Though he admired the stick's hickory,
Taking the money from the staff 's core,
Giving Ruby Lain her paltry sum and more,
Charging Eddie Pons for taking court time
In an attempt to perpetrate a crime—

Bob: K-plot! K-plot! K-plot!
Abruptly, the van rocked from side to side,
Felt like we hit a washboard ten feet wide,
We smelled burning rubber, k-plot! k-plot!
The right rear tire wobbled; it was shot,
The backend flipped sideways in a fishtail,
Shaking, taking the van on a random trail.
I white-knuckled the steering wheel, thinking,
"Whoa, steady as you go, no time for blinking,
Have to slow this crazy, crowded van down,
Before it tips onto its cushy crown."
Foot off the gas, I eased the van to the side,
The shoulder was graveled and plenty wide,
The veering van came to a shaking stop
As the blowout made a final k-plop.

Dr. Johnson took charge, she rode shotgun,
"Listen up, boys, this can be work or fun,
We've got a tire busted at the seam,
We can change her fast, if we work as a team.
Smokey and Bob will change the tire,
Virgil, Lupe, set up the flares for fire,

Place them twenty feet away from the van,
Buster, Lawrence watch traffic best you can.
T. Osprey, you best be handling the jack,
Raise the van; after we're done, set her back,
Lolo, Tom you bring the spare to Bob,
Okay, you boys, hustle up! Do your job."
Wasn't long before the team was churning,
The flares were in place and brightly burning,
The jack went under the van and raised it high,
While Buster and Tom sang with plenty of spry:
Shaw-naw-náw-naw. Shaw-naw-náw-naw.
They tapped, clapped, and sang in nonsense rime,
Keeping us moving in synchronized time
Just like workers of old who sang to make
Boring work fun for its own sake.
The spare mounted, the blowout put away,
In no time flat, we were back on our way.
Say what you will of the weaker gender,
Inger was the leader, the top contender,
She led us boys in a common cause,
Getting the job done right, without a pause,
We were back on the asphalt road again,
Without dispute among kith or kin.

6

INGER MAINLY MENTIONS MALE MANNERS

When the villagers battle over a jackass,
Loretta "Lori" Branch intervenes with pizzazz,
Thereto, the case of good teacher J.J. Brooks,
Who gambles and sins like other crooks,
Showing love with its many faces
Popping up in a poem and other places.
Tall tales, too, by Buster and T. Osprey,
Of perilous plights of animals born free.

Bob: Dr. Inger Johnson, former law school student,
For whom the practice of law just wasn't prudent,
Became a "Kitty Lit" librarian,
And a fabulous, feminist contrarian.
She's not a man-hater by any means,
And prefers to dress up in their jeans,
She's a take-charge kind of gal with her peers,
Getting the job done well without copious tears,
Inger, just now you whipped us into shape,
You're a can-do woman—that takes the cake!

Inger: You know, it was a gift of my mother's,
She put me in charge of my brothers,
Teddy bears, all four of them, two years apart,
And like you boys, independent and smart.
When Mother asked them to do big jobs,
Bigger than wiping and washing up daubs,
In macho-style each would work alone,
Working hard and getting tired to the bone,

Instead of coordinating like a team,
Each tried to do it all! It's a male thing.
You're right about my being a law student,
But for me, the study of law wasn't prudent,
Holy moly, during class I never heard a word
About justice, either as a noun or a verb,
Therefore, I sought to refocus my career,
Where I wouldn't have to watch my derrière.
But Bobby boy, it isn't legitimate
To say I'm a librarian of 'kitty lit,'
That trivializes what we've come to know
As the literature of children as they grow.
I decided to study children's literature,
So as to become involved in their future,
To introduce kids to morality and justice,
Which weighs heavy for the future of all of us.
As a girl, I would often curl up and read books,
Of rogues and crooks, your average Captain Hooks,
That's when I discovered a very male thing,
Men really like to fight, to wallop, and to sling,
As in this tale adapted from Don Qui-ho-tee,
I hope you like, but we shall see.

The Battle of the Brays

One bright night in July it came to pass,
Two villages were cooking up the gas,
To do war to maim and hurt each other,
A sad scene of brother against brother.
In stepped peacemaker, Loretta "Lori" Branch,
Who raised breeding bulls on a nearby ranch.
She was at supper of green beer and beans,
As was the custom of women of her means,

When she heard of the impending village war
And poked about to find out more.

It seems the village mayor of Plover
Had lost his donkey outside the clover,
That is, the donkey had wandered away
Into the deep woods, away from its stay.

The mayor went into the thick forest
And began to bray with hearty zest:

"E-haw! E-haw! Jack-a-a-s-s! Jack-a-a-s-s!"
Before long, twenty Jennies came en masse,
All had been lost in the forest thick
And extracting them was no easy trick.
Hey, that hardy, handy Polver mayor
Was one heck of a good donkey brayer!
His reputation spread throughout the land.
He brayed so donkeys could understand
To follow the belching burps of his bray,
From the thick woods to where it's okay.
Before long, the villagers in Midvale
Heard all about the braying mayor's hale,
Every time they spotted a Plover rube,
They'd belch-out a "he-haw" platitude:

"*E-haw! E-haw!*" How they blurted out mocks,
Grieving the Plover rubes down to their socks.
To fix this dishonorable situation,
The Plover men did a desecration,
Not on the mission chapel in Midvale,
They put donkey do-do in the village pail,
The bucket folks used at the Midvale well
To extract water by the Angelus bell.

Men in both villages were like knights,
Conscientious about making fights,
For both villages perceived an undue slam,
By the braying hecklers, or the do-do scam.
Both were inflicted an indignity,
Caused, each claimed, by the other's cupidity,
But, as a matter of fact, as a rule,
They both relished the chance to have a duel.

As I said, like knights they arranged to fight
Believing that the winner is in the right.

They soon agreed on a battle scene
In an empty meadow half-way between
The villages to fight for their honor,
One side would win, the other a goner.
Lori Branch reckoned the site of the fight,
And immediately geared up and took flight,
To intercede to try to stop the fray,
To let the men stay and play another day.

When she came to the designated meadow,
Already threats were flowing to and fro,
The yokels were lined-up in crooked rows,
Building up courage to throw some blows.
Don't get me wrong, these men were true knights,
Bent on fighting to aggrieve their gripes,
Both sides were equipped with shovels and hoes,
With little else, no swords, spears, or crossbows.
(Granted, their weapons weren't state-of-the-arts,
Yet, their foul words maimed the hardest hearts.)

Lori slipped between the mangy mobs,
And shouted, "¡Alto! Stop! You craven cobs,

Abort this plot to battle to the death
By stopping to rest and taking a breath."
The two sides were suddenly very still
As though they'd taken a sleeping pill,
For among the warring beasts, chirped a lark,
In the brave tradition of Joan of Arc.
Lori continued to make her appeal,
Although her voice revealed a squeamish squeal,
While she maneuvered mostly to mediate
Between the brayers and them who desecrate:

"Now tell me, honest, you of Christian zeal,
Why do you plan to do war and to kill?"
The villagers from Plover spoke up first,
Who, in deed, believed
                    they were aggrieved the worst:
"Folks from Midvale dishonored our mayor,
Poking fun at our outstanding brayer."

Lori asked, "men of Midvale, what of this charge?
Tell the truth, nothing but the truth, don't enlarge."

" *E-haw, e-haw* is all that we shouted,"
Quipped the Midvalers, "and they went and pouted,
Placing blame on us is certainly crass
Just because their mayor brays like a jackass."

Then again, the Midvalers reversed and said:
"Who bewitched Plover men? What got in their head
To put the donkey do-do in our pail
And sully our drinking water without fail?
It was the Plover men who gave insult,
And this bloody war will be the result."

Lori knew she must do something quick,
Before somebody started to kick,
So she shouted, "war is really absurd!
Nothing more than the instincts of the herd!
All of you yokels should take a good look
At what is said of war in the *Good Book*:
All the mighty rivers run into the sea,
Yet, the sea is not full—all is vanity.
Don't you get it? Making war is in vain,
Though you act in the name of raising Cain. "

"You know this bray battle is back-ass-wards,
It's mainly malarkey and for the birds,
You who complain of do-do in your pail
Could buy a new one at a flea market sale.
And, you proud men of the village of Plover,
Who can't take a joke about your top drover,
Think about it, almost anyone can bray,
Especially when it's done this way."
She lowered her head and stuck-out her butt
To emulate a donkey, and not for smut,
She rested her arms on her hips akimbo,
Projecting to all a donkey bimbo,
Then, she brayed and brayed out loud,
Wiggling her butt before the crowd.

She pivoted so that every man there
Heard the brays and saw her wiggles, as a pair:
"E-haw! E-haw! E-haw! Swish-Swish.
E-haw! E-haw! E-haw! Swish-Swish."
On each "Swish-Swish," her butt wiggled the crowd,
Much, much more than the crowd allowed.

"Big butt! Big butt! You low down scum,
How dare you swish us, you crazy crumb!"
The vocal yokels joined without a sword
To poke, pinch, and punch Lori in accord.

Lori rued, "are you mad 'cuz I'm uncouth,
Or, are you mad 'cuz I told the truth?"

Suddenly, they stopped berating Loretta
As their passion petered-out for vendetta,
They organized into small, gabby groups
And disbanded the large, leery troops.
In their small groups, they reviewed the *Good Book,*
How it wouldn't hurt to take a second look
At the foolish men who shouted the bad jokes,
And the men offended by the silly pokes.
Lori managed with her ludicrous call
To unite the villagers, who did recall
The intent to do battle, to quit the fight,
To wrangle with words all through the night.
Blessed be the peacemakers, one and all,
For their pleas to placate men in the mall.

All: Amen!

Smokey: Inger, you've got one idea right,
Quite a few men really like to fight.

Buster: Smokey, that's not the whole truth, a'tall,
Most men go to war when they're given the call,
Most would rather be home with their families,
Instead of dodging bullets behind the trees.

Inger: I think it's built into your genes
To be effective war machines,
From way back when, the days of the cave,
When men had to guard their nave.

Virgil: We stepped from the cave *beau coup* years ago,
And learned we only crack our hearts and soul
When we wage war, which makes more men dead
Without solving problems in its stead.
Nowadays, the idea of war itself
Has been whitewashed and placed on the shelf
As a sterile, sanitary affair,
To where people are duped and aren't aware
Of *smart* bombs and their collateral damage—
No one's killed. There's only the excess baggage
Of human bodies that get in the way
Of smart bombs that *never* go astray.

Lawrence: Peace is not an alternative to war,
It's a cause, a consequence, and much more
Than absence of war. We have to be willing
To engage in talk rather than killing.
Haven't you noticed how good we are
At building bombs and shooting them far?
Haven't you noticed how poor we are
At building bonds at par?

Lolo: As our population increases,
And the space for living decreases,
We'll have to find a rational way
To control population growth and decay,
Time-honored methods, include making war,
With famine and disease to even the score,
But, do we want to use these anymore?

Inger: Go figure, war does lower population,
Now that we have the bomb, and its radiation,
Modern man, most likely, may have the distinction
Of being responsible for his own extinction.

T. Osprey: We shouldn't put too much stock
In all this pessimistic talk,
And, we shouldn't make much room
For theorems of gloom and doom.

Virgil: Sometimes, we should give peace a chance,
Like in your tale of peacemaker, Lori Branch,
With warfare, there's nothing new under the sun,
The mighty get their way with a germ or gun.
If Thomas Aquinas were here today,
He'd have plenty of plethora to say:
War is wrong, wrong, wrong, wrong.

Lupe: Sometimes, we have no choice but to fight,
To intercede and use all of our might,
There are morally justifiable wars
For self-defense and to settle old scores.

Buster: War, for self-defense, I agree,
To settle old scores, I disagree,
Sometimes folks fight to settle the score,
But they've forgotten why they're sore.

Inger: Then, there's the case of a man who forgot
That the social contract is part of our lot,
Like Larry, it's a case I can't erase
That we studied during law school days.
Larry, on law I'll defer to you,

Who had the patience to finish law school,
If I get any legal matters wrong,
Go ahead and chime-in, as I go along.

Lawrence: Okay, but I sure hate to spoil
                          Your chance to rant and roil.

Virgil: Ho! Ho! Don't worry, my good man,
She'll sock it to us whenever she can.

Inger: Ho! Ho! It's sure man of you
To defend *this* motor pool!
Everybody now, listen well,
As I take my second turn to tell.

Jeremy J. Brooks, Principal-Teacher

Not every lawsuit involves rogues and crooks,
Some just involve plain, ordinary folks,
Like the case of Jeremy Jay Brooks
Who imbibed nothing stronger than cokes.
J.J. Brooks was one of those good teachers
Respected for his common sense scruples,
Honesty and patience were his features
To deal with seriously sassy pupils.

He knew each by temperament and name,
So as to affect their soul and mind,
Never allowed excuses that were lame,
And he liked ideas of any kind.

Well, wasn't long he was named principal
For he worked with students and parents well,
Toiling night and day without a lull,

Paying no mind to time clock or bell.

Soon, he forgot about his home and wife,
And soon she left him to wander astray,
Seeking a much more exciting life
Than one when the spouse is always away.
Mr. Brooks continued his gentle, good works,
Tending to the teachers and students,
Running the school with regal rewards and perks,
Insisting on common sense and prudence.

Come every July, Brooks was free to play,
He was off-duty and could vacation,
Being lonely, he went Nevada-way
To gamble and frolic in prostitution,

Playing stud poker and rolling dice,
Yanking one-arm bandits, losing his coins,
Consorting with girls who were nice for a price,
And depleting his pocket book and loins.

One August when Brooks returned to his school,
He was given a letter of dismissal
For his July affairs where he played the fool,
Breaking the *Educator's Epistle*,
And the laws of Utah, the Zion State,
Which forbids all sins against God and man,
For people who gamble and fornicate,
He was fired for breaking the ban.

"You can't can me," Brooks claimed, "I'll tell you why,
Down Nevada-way, gambling and whoring
Are legal so long as you do comply

With the rules of the house, which are goring!
Besides, in July I was footloose free,
Without any contract bindings or mandates
To keep me from frivolity and spree,
To vacation without restraints or gates.
This accusation is a real bummer,
How do any of you really know
How I spent my free time in the summer?
Did anyone see me spending my dough?"

It was the President of the School Board,
Who went to the same place as J.J. Brooks,
He was a tort lawyer and could afford
To gamble and hang with a girl that hooks.
Now, he went there for the same thing,
There was little difference with these two guys,
The President was married and wore a ring,
Claimed his July jaunts were boldface lies.
This case is not as simple as it looks,
What do you think about good teacher Brooks?

Lolo: We can't expect Brooks to be a priest,
Especially when he's off-contract, at least.

Smokey: Yet, he owes more to the community
    Than just domestic notoriety.

Lupe: What of the *Educator's Epistle*,
Giving grounds for a teacher's dismissal?

Lawrence: When a teacher is tenured or first hired,
There are reasons why he can be fired,
Reason of incompetence is the first,
But, that reason is by no means the worst.

Immorality is the most dire
To put your livelihood on the wire,
In fact, immorality is the most grim,
Anyone can be charged and found to sin.
If guilty of an immoral act,
Say goodbye to your teaching contract.

T. Osprey: What about the lawyer guy?
Does anyone wonder why
He wants to fire Jay Brooks?
In this case, who are the crooks?

Inger: This case is on a much higher plane
Than man-made laws dealing with the profane.
Teaching our children is a sacred trust,
Which mandates a higher standard, we must
Accept no behavior less than the best,
Schooling calls for a higher moral test.
People who teach buy into a contract,
A sacred covenant they can't retract
To serve as role models for their students,
Who need ideal adults to show prudence,
Adults to imitate and emulate,
When their time comes to work and procreate.

Lawrence: J.J. Brooks was just a regular guy,
Who worked very hard and played on the sly,

He is most certainly correct to say,
He broke no laws in Utah; he shouldn't pay
By losing his job as principal-teacher,
He's just a misunderstood creature.

Inger: With teacher Brooks, the law is of little use,
He broke the sacred trust, there's no excuse,
Nor are there laws for him to hide behind,
It's a moral issue of the highest kind.
As for his hypocritical accuser,
He's nothing but a low-down, first class loser,
A horny toad, who should behave for teachers
At a standard you would set for preachers.
The Board fired Brooks as immoral,
Forcing him to leave town without laurel,
Unable to work in schools again,
But, the Board President moved to Michigan,
Wherein he still practices law by day,
What he does during the night, who can say?

Virgil: Brooks looked for love in the wrong place,
I mean paying cash for sex is so base,
Love should be an act of freedom without reins,
And for the lovers, there should be no pains.
Imagine you're walking a wooded path,
A shower has given the flowers a bath,
And you come across daisies budding wild,
Each a sprightly, saucy, spunky child,
Beads of raindrops are spattered on the plants,
Nolens volens! You fall into a trance,
For you're struck by one lovely daisy there,
Beaming, blooming, blossoming, oh, so fair.
You notice its frisky, fresh white petals,
And its buds in the hues of precious metals,
That daisy is to you—a beam of sunshine,
A breath of fresh air, a carafe of fine wine,
You're in love with that beautiful daisy
And don't care if people think you're crazy.

Do you pluck the daisy to take it home
And put it in a vase to call your own?
Do you uproot it for others to see,
Or, do you leave that lovely daisy be?

Lupe: E-ho! Virgil, you cagey old fox,
You've raised a perplexing paradox,
If you're selfish with love, it will surely die,
You'll be left alone to sit and cry,
To pine away feeling sorry for yourself
For trying to bottle beauty on a shelf.

Smokey: Getting out of the paradox is not hard,
Why, I'd transplant the daisy to my yard,
Where it could bloom and blossom, oh, so fair,
And anyone could see it without fare.

Tom: Jeez Louise, am I the one who's hazy?
I don't get it, this talk of the daisy,
What does it have to do with teacher Brooks
Who hangs with a shady lady who hooks?

T. Osprey: For classroom teachers, I remember when,
There was a double standard for women and men,
It was okay for the guys to go to pubs,
Or, get drunk and sloppy at supper clubs,
If a woman frequented a club or pub,
She was in trouble, and her name was mud.

Inger: We've struggled for that day to be long gone,
When *Juana* was treated worse than your *Don Juan,*
So here's a below-the-belt blow,

It's solely Brooks' fault he fell so low.
He should've been at Summer Institutes,
Instead of spending Julys with prostitutes,
Makes no sense to make Brooks a treatise on love,
When you look at the facts, discussed above,
I think Virgil's paradox is a *non sequitur,*
What do you think, Lawrence, do you concur?

Lawrence: The issue is not, is he guilty or not,
He should've never allowed to get caught,
Thereby turning into a loose cannon,
Violating the Good Ol' Boys canon:
"It's okay to gamble and raise a fuss,
Just don't get caught and embarrass us."
All of the charges should have been denied,
Alleging that the accuser had lied,
Saying the accuser had a grudge on him,
Or, the accuser fabricated a whim.
Once Brooks came clean and embarrassed us,
Absolving him would cause a raucous ruckus,
Especially with the ladies like Inger,
All too ready to point the finger
At us men, and our complicated codes,
Condoning the horny behavior of toads.

Buster: What happened to J.J. really stunk,
And, I can't agree all laws are bunk,
Because there are laws we can't control
No matter how hard we guard or patrol.

Hunting a Doe and Her Fawn

Last autumn when I went out hunting deer,
In my path, a doe and her fawn drew near,

I had found their pine-needled nesting home,
The doe and the fawn lived there all alone,
They were returning from getting a drink
Down in a draw in a bushy sink.
I quickly aimed my rifle at the doe
Without a thought of worry or woe,
I squeezed the trigger. Wumppf! She fell, dying,
My eyes were watering, I was crying
For the tottering fawn as he ambled on
Into the woods and the fading dawn.
Durnedest thing, the fawn turned to stare at my gun,
Wondering where such a force would come from,
It was me, not the gun, that was the source
That triggered an irreversible course.

The fawn would not survive by his lonesome,
For I killed his mother, I was the bum,
The law of nature is very, very clear,
To live, a baby needs its mother near.

Inger: So, hey, go figure! Why'd you pull the trigger?
You should have picked on someone bigger.

Buster: It was the predator's instinct, I reckon,
That propped me to take the beckon.

Inger: Man, oh man, what is it with you guys,
After the fact and the act, you get wise?
All your crocodile tears, gnashing of teeth
Won't call back the doe...or the fawn's grief.

Lupe: Go easy on friend Buster,
It took him a lot to muster

A confession that he cries,
Among us guys, that's not wise.
And besides, don't feel sorry for the fawn,
He'll do fine as he goes along.

T. Osprey: Wild animals aren't helpless creatures,
In fact, one of their admirable features
Is they know how to take care of themselves,
Although they appear to be like elves,
Sort of cute and adorable, but yet,
You really can't adopt them as a pet.
Still yet, each animal is a perfect being,
When it comes to sensing, smelling, and seeing,
The imperfect animals just don't last,
Mother Nature wipes them out pretty fast,
It's a tough test only the fittest survive,
Judging by those who manage to stay alive.

Don't Mess With Buffalo Gals

Once when I ventured to Yellowstone Park,
On a leisurely trip, mostly a lark,

I spied a small, baby buffalo
Playing alone, or I thought that was so.
He was in a meadow, surrounded by trees,
Romping and rolling on his back, taking his ease.
I snuck closer to have a better see,
Stalking him, I crouched nearer tree-to-tree,
Till I found myself in the open field
To where I could see how the baby's build.
He was a cute bugger, all rusty brown,
Rolling around in the grass like a clown.

Here's where I learned my lesson, dear brothers,
About stepping between babies and mothers,
My mistake was, I got as close as can be
When I noticed a cow had her eye on me.
All-a-sudden! She charged to where I was
Moving faster than a lightning does,
I turned to run from that buffalo cow,
Running as fast as I could and knew how,
Still yet, she kept gaining ground on me fast,
Closing the gap on my lap, I was aghast,
When wham! I ran into a dead-standing tree,
And fell down, stars spinning around me,
My chest burned with an excruciating pain,
I couldn't run or walk; I couldn't feign.
The cow was still running to where I sat,
I clawed up the dead tree like a lame cat,
O-O-O! Each time I pulled,
   pain shot through my chest,
Like prickly cactus jabbing my breast,
O-O-O! E-E-E! How it hurt as I climbed,
Yet, for me, the cow had a worse pain in mind,
She kept banging the tree trunk with her head,
If I gave up and fell down, I'd be dead,
If she knocked the tree over, I would fall, too,
And that would'a been the end of this here fool.
She finally tired and went away,
Kind of *kiboshing* my Yellowstone stay,
I slid down the tree and crawled to my car,
It was close by, but the pain made it seem far.

I crawled, and rested, and crawled for a long time,
Though the pain couldn't be numbed with scotch or
wine,

I pulled myself onto the driver's seat,
That's the last thing I recall, really beat....
An angler came when he heard my horn
And found me slumped on it, passed out and forlorn,
He took me to the Yellowstone Hospital
Where a dour doctor posed a riddle:
"What kind of professor is such a dumb-dumb,
To come between a buffalo and her young one?"
You know the answer to the question, pals,
Don't ever mess with buffalo gals!

Inger: You're lucky you got away
Before that cow had her say.

T. Osprey: Doc said I was lucky to be going home
With bruises and a broken collar bone,
Man-o-mighty, it could'a been much worse
To be taken home in a hulking hearse.
Lemme tell one more Yellowstone tale
So's I can warm up for my turn to rail.

All: Way to go!
Dos-à-dos,

Futile Fray and Play

A kingpin bull elk convenes his harem
And travels down to the grassy canyon floor,
Where early snow hasn't yet fallen
And his hungry harem can graze once more.
That's when the kingpin's big troubles begin,
When another old bull elk confronts him

To battle over the harem to rule,
But, he's got to butt-out the kingpin bull.
(Overall, the most aggressive rule,

This applies to old bull elk, too.)
Acting out on a primordial ken,
The second old bull brashly horns-in!

Both butt heads, their racks clank and clatter
In a harried, headstrong battle to rule
As the young bull elk assess the matter,
Watching and waiting for the timely clue
To mate a cow while the old bulls batter.
(Overall, the most aggressive rule,
This applies to young bull elk, too.)
That is, during the heat of the old bulls' fight,
A younger bull elk will bleat a bugle
To tempt-out a cow to mate outright,
But, if none come, and the bugle's futile,
He'll jump to hump a cow, as a right.
The coy cow may not put up a spat,
Which would surely surprise the younger bull,
More likely, she would spat—tit-for-tat,
As he plays to pass on his gene pool.
(Overall, the most aggressive rule,
This applies to young bull elk, too.)

Good for me, there's an alternate way
To pass on and perpetuate my gene pool,
For when I count the number of cows that stay
With the bull elk that fights to win and rule,
My puny gene pool wouldn't stay to play,

Or frantically flay away at futile fray.
Most likely, it would be dinner in a wolf 's den,
Where the pack would rip it apart, limb-from-limb,
The wolves, too, acting on a primordial ken
To fill their bellies as winter sets in.
(Overall, the most aggressive rule,
This applies to young and old bull elk, too.)

Inger: T. Osprey, don't worry a bit,
There'll be plenty who are smit
By what you have to offer,
It's more than fishing that you confer.

Virgil: After hearing about laws, cases, and chases,
I believe that I have much more of a basis
To say that the truth is much harsher than fiction,
For what it's worth, that's my predilection.

Bob: Well, well. We can all plainly see
Inger cleared the path for good friend, T. Osprey.

7

T. Osprey Tantalizes with Theorems on Fishing

Of the plain vain trout fishing theorem,
And for Uncle Bill there is no serum
When he gets bit in the mouth by a fake,
Instead of a worm, he'd mouthed a snake.
Smokey tells of how tricky Old Man Coyote
Helps trout get a colorful, rainbow coat,
T. Osprey shows he has a blue side
By telling of the sad way one osprey died,
After he recites an ode to earthworms,
Known in 'hoods and 'burbs for artful berms.

Bob: We should receive for better or worser,
T. Osprey Munsch as a new professor,
He teaches with a constructivist approach,
Claims it's above and beyond reproach:
You put your hands on a problem to figure,
Then you try to solve it, or reconfigure.
The method purports to use the real thing
Without allowing for Pavlov's ding-a-ling,
The inert students are compelled to think,
Weigh and consider solutions, or sink.
Well, Professor, if you are up to it,
Let's hear your promise to be a poet.

T. Osprey: I will advance my rainbow trout theory,
  Hoping by now that you're not too weary.

The Plain Vain Trout Thesis

Now that I've completed my dissertation
In elementary science education,
I will discourse about trout from my heart
Served up in a dish not too bland or tart,
To shape the theorem I will use a rule
Of logic I learned in graduate school—
In the main, trout are vain.

Consider this theory based on more than hunch,
My thesis—T. Fishes Like Osprey Munsch,
Who after much menial mediation,
And meandering meditation
Can show to have derived what's beyond doubt
The aquatic nature of that gull durned trout.
Some say trout like the water cool and running,
Others say, you've got to be more cunning
To know when trout prefer night crawlers, grubs,
Corn, live worms, or itty-bitty bugs.

It's important to note, on reflection,
Trout have some built-in crap food detection,
They won't bite or snatch a jigger-bug
Made from the handle of a plastic jug.
They're not fast food junkies, by any means,
Preferring raw grubs and worms for their proteins,
They're not bottom stream sucker-huggers,
When it comes to olive, woolly buggers,

But, it's true. They're impatient and can't wait
To glom onto a corn and cheese power bait—
In the main, trout are vain.

I guess some strategizing is okay,
Although you're not listening to what I say,
When it comes to science and trout fishing,
There's sufficient shibboleth and wishing,
But, there's only one thing you've got to know
If you want to see your trout-record grow—
In the main, trout are vain.

When all is strategized, studied and done,
And you've figured all ways under the sun,
When you've reckoned their habitual habitat,
And separated the scum from the scat,
When you've checked your line and cast your bait,
And are ready, willing, and able to wait,

I'm telling you again, it's more than hunch,
This thesis of T. Fishes Like Osprey Munsch—
In the main, trout are vain.
In toto, rainbow trout are incurably vain,

Why they even presume a Latin name,
Oncorhynchus mykiss is what they're called,
It's what makes them so doggone self-enthralled,
Even though they're not salmon, whales, or sharks,
It's enough for them to light their sparks.
At last, when your line is out cast,
You're patiently waiting for a bite, at last,
You shouldn't even tend to your line at all,
Much better to let it slope, slack and fall,

You've got to pretty well pretend a bit,
So the trout will think you don't give a spit—
In the main, trout are vain.

It doesn't matter, really, what you do,
I swear on a six-pack of *Coors*, it's true,
You can jump around or mumble a song,
Even map miles from here to Hong Kong,
'Cuz if you ignore trout in the least bit,
You'll be sure to catch more than your limit.
I can tell by the glazed gleam in your eyes,
You're wondering why I tell craven lies,
So here's my full thesis when it's writ—
You catch your limit, if you don't give a spit,
In the main, trout are vain.

Bob: That's one to appeal to every feller,
Not sure it will be a million seller,
Most every fish story tries to convey
The struggle of how the big one got away.

T. Osprey: How you handle the struggle counts
When you're balancing your fishing accounts.
One of the best fish stories ever told
Is about anglers when they grow old,
They dream of lions and deeds of their youth,
Till the fish jerks their line somewhat uncouth,
Dragging them out into the deep, blue sea,
Far from their hut on a Cuban lea.

Lawrence: You refer to *Old Man and the Sea,*
A tale of the highest degree,
Tells of how old men fade away,
The best of Papa Hemingway.

T. Osprey: One thing an angler knows
Is that any gull durn theory goes.

If you're pragmatic as all get-out,
You'll catch fish by fin or snout,
For if nothing else is understood,
If you're catchin'em, your theory's good.

Virgil: Not so fast! Don't be too sure of that,
I hate to nit-pick like a bureaucrat,
In Herman Melville's book, *Moby Dick,*
The whale caught the captain without a trick,
Ahab lured the whale close to his harpoon,
Wasn't long, Ahab was in a monsoon,
Where the whale snared him and pulled him under,
The fish caught him…makes you wonder.

T. Osprey: Reminds me of fishing for the Muskie
In Wisconsin near Lake Poniatowski,
Where they bait with pieces of two-by-fours,
Rotten roots, broken blades, auger bores
And other lures you can't find in stores.
Four weeks wasted, fishing the murky Muskie,
Found out I was just another wannabe,
For I was hooked on landing a Muskie,
But no Muskie was hooked on letting me.
As for that fanatic Captain Ahab guy,
He was bit by the bug, the urge to try
To harpoon the biggest fish of them all,
Hubris, I'd say, was his downfall.

Bob: Have you done any of your research
On the tricks to catch mud cats or perch?
And, what of the art of fly fishing,
Do your theories go beyond wishing?

T. Osprey: Now you're into cross-cultural instruction,
For which I make very little presumption,
If you don't know the culture of cats and perch,
You might as well spend Sunday in church.
As for the art of catching fish by fly,
I've not the qualifications to try,
For I do all my angling with live bait,
Or anything else you can marinate.
Fly fishermen think of themselves to be
A notch higher than fishermen like me,
Status never bothered me or Uncle Bill,
Who fished with live bait and a spinning reel.

Uncle Bill's Live Bait

When it comes to fishing rainbow trout,
Uncle Bill had a theory pungent and stout,
Liter'ly, he had a theory that stunk,
Due mostly to a big tobacco chunk,
And his breath, pee-yew! So stinky it would kill
Any chance of making a sweet deal.
In the afternoon before he'd go fishin',
He'd mix a curmudgeon's concoction
Blending a giant cud of tobacco
With *Grey Poupon* and peppered *Tabasco*,
Which he chewed all evening the night long,
Though my Aunt Cele wasn't that strong.
She made Uncle Bill sleep on the couch,
Course, he took it in stride, he was no grouch.

Next morning, he'd go to where he kept worms
Without thinking much about getting germs,

He would grab the fat worms that were about,
And put those fat wiggly worms in his mout'.
He did use the worms bred by George Sroda,
Who's known from Texas to Minnesota,
For breeding the most juicy succulent worms
That even meet USDA concerns
Over fatty content and lean, red meat,
For catching rainbow trout, they can't be beat.
(In Wisconsin, George is known as the *Worm Czar,*
With *Herman the Worm,* he really went far,
He's expert on the nightcrawler and redworm,
Read his pithy books, if you want to learn.)

Back to Unc. He'd drive to Trout Haven Lake
Where there were a few trout on the take,
It wasn't long after just a few throws
That his creel basket bulged with rainbows.
Now, Uncle Bill thought he was pretty slick,
Keeping the worms in his mouth did the trick,
Because rainbows like breakfast fat and warm,
And the tobacco coated his mouth from harm.
One day he came home late to Aunt Cele,
Shaking, burning a fever, he was ill,
He felt worse than a sick cow with slobbers,
So bad, in fact, he'd forgot his bobbers—
Something seriously wrong with ole Unc,
He was shaking like a cold turkey drunk.

Aunt Cele could tell he was plenty sick,
So she took him to Dr. Fuller quick,
You won't believe it, just leave it to Doc,
He said Uncle Bill suffered venom shock.

"I'll be!" wailed Uncle Bill and up he sat,
"One of them juicy worms was mighty fat,
I took him 'cuz he had plenty of lard,
Bet he's the one that bit my tongue so hard."
By now you can infer what happened is,
A baby snake got in those worms of his.

Bob: You're full of stuff as a Christmas turkey,
And one thing I like better than jerky
Is to listen to hear your cock-and-bull,
You're full of it, you know? You're full.

Tom: Gee T, that George Sroda earthworm guy
Must'a fallen from a wormhole in the sky.

T. Osprey: Ah, George, when in a poetic mode,
Would worm prosaic on an earthy ode
About the segmented, lowly earthworm,
A.K.A., the nightcrawler, grass, and dew-worm.

Ode to an Earthworm
Some fugle folks say dog is man's best friend,
I say the earthworm will soon take this trend,
He pokes hard, sod clods like he had spiked boots,
Permitting air and water to reach the roots,

He grinds rocks in his powerful gizzard,
Much better than a chicken or bird,
Adding fertilizer to the soil
Without costing us a cent of toil.
Some folks say a worm is a squirmy thing,
Who would if he could, take writhing wing,

That he's only good to use as fish bait,
Due to his skinny body and low weight.
Beyond meeting the baiting wishes
Of Brooks, Browns, and all them that fishes,
The earthworm's used with pills and herbs
By many hospitals in 'hoods and 'burbs,
He's used for fixing fine foods and pop-art,
With non-toxic paint, he squirms quite a chart.
He's of the *annelid* class of earthworms,
Who writhes, wiggles, and wends in balmy berms,
After a spring shower, take a look around,
You'll see winding, worm-whorls on the ground:
To wit, this whorl looks like a tasty tomato,
That one, the spiral of a tornado,
Another like Picasso's nude
Descending stairs with an angular dude,
This one, like ancient hieroglyphic lines,
Others like spires in the tall, tall pines.
Some call this worm a *Rivershore Walker,*
And granted, he's not much of a talker,
If he could talk, I'm sure he would say
He's useful in a basic sort of way.

Smokey: On night crawlers
            George had plenty to say,
I'm not sorry he got carried away,
Sure, night crawlers are known for artful berms,
Though best known for ecological concerns,
They play a silent part in nature's features
And are still scorned as slithery creatures.

T. Osprey: Then there's the giant Palouse earthworm
Of blubber-like flesh though firm,

Its body is clear as a plastic straw
Showing all the organs of its tiny maw,
Ten to twelve inches long when fully grown
Of clear flesh, organs, and not a single bone.
Its head is dappled in a pretty pink,
Collared at the neck in a yellowish ink,
At the other end, it trails a bulbous tail
Rounded like a Brussels sprout or kale.
It has produced iffy, trifling myths
Causing rare riffs and tiny tiffs,
About smelling like Easter lilies
And spitting dirt as far as it sees.

Smokey: Enough on worms. Here's a tale
Of how the trout came to be so hale,
Old Man Coyote played an important part
Giving the Rainbow Trout a start.

How Trout Got Rainbow Coats

Long before Rainbow Trout had such a name,
Inland trout looked pretty much the same,
Okay, sure, you could find certain Cutthroats,
Brooks and Browns swimming medieval moats,
But as far back as trout history goes,
There just weren't any colorful rainbows,
Not until Old Man Coyote pulled his prank,
According to Henry Realbird, old friend Hank.

To Old Man Coyote, all trout were just fish,
All the same to catch and fry for his dish,
Thus, he devised a tricky game real neat
To catch him some yummy fishes to eat:

First of all, he built a huge bonfire
To fry the yummy fish in a pyre,
They'd soon slide into a large tin can
That he'd concocted into a frying pan.
Second of all, he found a tall waterfall,
With water cascading down its wall,
Causing a pretty rainbow to exist
As the falling water rose in a mist.
Third, he grabbed one of the rainbow's end,
Bending and twisting it so it would wend
To form a direct path, like twisted wire,
That ended at Old Man Coyote's fire.
(At one end of the rainbow was a pool
At the other end, if the story's true,
Was a fire and pan ready to cook
Any trout that swam-up the rainbow brook.)

Fourth, he returned to the waterfall pool,
Where he howled a tune that was really cool,
Standing right close, beside the water bank,
He crooned a tune, giving the young fish a yank:
"Hey-y-y-y-ya! All you youn-n-n-ng trout,
Com-m-over! Swim up the rain-n-n-bow route,
Where you can swim-m-m-m up to the very top,
Then tumble back down in the pool—ker-r-r-rplop!"

Some of the young trout were easy to fool
Because the rainbow route sounded cool,
So right off, some young trout started up,
Not knowing they'd be Old Man Coyote's sup.

At the top, they fell down,
      down,
            down they'd go,
Sliding down the fire-side of the rainbow,
Slipping down to where the rainbow wended
Into a frying pan where the rainbow ended,
There, they all lay down, frying side-by-side
In an unintended kind of suicide.
Now Mizfish gave the rainbow game a try,
But she didn't want to bake or fry,
So she paced herself, swimming ever so slow
As she swam up the arc of the rainbow.

There she looked down to where the rainbow ends,
Where in a frying pan, she could see her friends.
She stopped, treading water at the top,
Then turned around in an agile flip-flop,
Wrapping the rainbow's mist around her skin,
Covering every part and every fin,
Rolling back into the water pool,
She wasn't Old Man Coyote's meal or fool.
The rainbow colors stuck to her as a coat
Wherever she'd swim in lake or moat.

T. Osprey: Smokey, that old story
Is as true as it can be,
Or, my name isn't T. Osprey!

Bob: I guess *T. Osprey's* not such a strange name,
When you consider the bird's fishing fame,
It's said with fishing, osprey are regal
And much faster than the eagle.

T. Osprey: As a raptor,
An osprey can capture
Whatever he preys after,
Very graceful and good at fishing,
He's got to be good to eat. There's no wishing.

Big Fish Catches Osprey

Once when I was lake fishing at Moose Creek,
While scrounging around to take a leak,
I spied a young osprey diving from a tree,
Aiming for a fish like a *kamikaze*.
Ker-plash! The osprey hit the water hard,
Surprising the feisty fish—his trump card,
Man-o-mighty, he snagged that fish so fine
As he grappled to fly from the water line.
The more he flapped his wings, the wetter they got
Till the osprey was sopped, like a drunken sot.
Once his talons gripped into that fat fish,
They were locked-on, no matter what his wish,
The osprey and fish were as tight as solder,
He couldn't let go, come hell or high water,
The big fish pulled him down into the lake,
Leaving a few, fluffed feathers in the wake....
We know that fish is still in the reservoir,
With the osprey hooked to it, and much more,
I know of anglers who lost their lines and hooks,
Snapped by that fish who's heavier than books.
Someday, some angler may bring that fat fish in
On a flashy lure with a flip-and-tin-spin,
In his mouth will be many hooks to see,
On his back, the skeleton of the osprey.

Virgil: Sort of reminds you of Captain Ahab,
Only for the osprey, it's much more sad,
The osprey was driven by the need to eat,
Ahab was driven by *hubris* and conceit.

Lolo: On fishing, no one can steal your thunder,
You ought to have a 1-800 number,
To sell bait fishing advice by the time,
Where and when do they bite? And, in what clime?
Or, a better promotion even yet,
Set-up a homepage on the Internet,
So anglers who troll the World-Wide-Web
Can locate fishes hiding in the ebb.

T. Osprey: There's a lure
    involving sardines and dough,
Concocted by nephew Juan from Colorado,
He borrowed the notion from his fishing dad,
Who taught Juan to fish when he was a lad.
In fact, his dad is my bigger brother,
Who angles with bait and lures like no other,
And I dare not tell tales about him,
Or he'll jam a fist-sandwich where I grin.
Enough said. Here's the lure invented by him:
Pop open a can of *Pillsbury* dough,
And ball the dough into a four-cup bowl;
Open a can of oil-packed sardines
And pour the oil and sardines, by any means,
Over the roll of dough, but don't wait
To marinate. Knead till you've got gooey bait.
(You can mix-in garlic or anise
For extra smells, they're effective, more-or-less.)

Mold a gob of dough onto a treble hook
And cast into a deep pond or shallow nook,
Soon a fish will glom onto your power bait,
As Isaac Walton's my judge,
    you won't have long to wait,
Sardines and dough, in clear water or hazy,
Will work. The sardine smell drives fish crazy.

Lawrence: Deep fried, you're recipe
sounds good to eat,
Later on, I may ask for a repeat.

T. Osprey: Now suppose I set up a WEB site
To sell this type of lore day and night,
I'd be working during my free time
To make a nickel, maybe a dime.
I'd have to record the FAXs,
Collect money, keep books, and pay taxes,
Taking the pleasure out of fishing
And depriving me of what I like dishing.
I'd rather have fun. I prefer to use email
And Web-based courses, letter grades or pass-fail,
Which I bait and fish during the year
In my courses on fishing jigs and gear.

Inger: No doubt, they are *avant-garde* courses,
From anchovy lures to zombie forces.

Bob: Inger, aren't you going to pull the stoppers
On all of T. Osprey's wacky whoppers?

Inger: Naw, why? T. Osprey is so bright,
He's a true-grit *Canonite*,

Were I young and without latch,
He'd be a hunky hatch to catch,

For him every night I would dish
A plate of his favorite fish,
So, na~aw, why sweat the small stuff?
The big stuff is tough enough.

T.Osprey: Cripes, I can't take too much credit,
There was a great Dame who first said it,
Said it first and best I would wrangle
In *Treatise of Fishing with an Angle*,
Published in 1496,
Providing gentlemen fishing tips,
Juliana Berners was her name
And fishing was her favorite game.

Inger: Hmm. A woman on fishing, you don't say,
First kept fishermen from going astray?

T. Osprey: Yep! I certainly do say,
With baits and flies, by the way.

Virgil: Well, I'm not much of a fishing wrangler,
What about Isaak Walton's *The Compleat Angler*?

T. Osprey: His 1653 pub to hers—1496,
She was the first in English on fishing tips,
Her book is a didactic treatise
Based on Solomon's 'good life' premise:
To live long, always keep a good thought,
Don't work much more than you ought,
Avoid quarrels or making a riot,
Be sure to eat a moderate diet,

And one way to keep a good thought,
Says Dame Berners, is to go fishing a lot.
That is, her treatise was a how-to-do-it-book,
Serving like a recipe book serves a cook.
It provides creel baskets of details
For fishing off river banks and pier rails,
Using a rod, line, floater, and hook,
If you're serious 'bout fishin', take a look
At the way she says to make a good rod
From pliant wood provided by Nature's God,
Or, make line with the hair of a horse's tail
Strong enough to catch all but a whale.
Also, she details data on baits and flies,
As a scientist, she was precise and concise.
Isaak Walton's book was in the obverse,
Describing fishing in song, prose, and verse
In the classic *belles-lettre* venue
Of fine art and aesthetic value.

Lawrence: Let's stop fishing and cut bait
To turn to a more timely debate,
When you go online, you should be discrete
As though speaking aloud on a crowded street,
Don't beam loose words to cause you grief and stress
When they're downloaded and printed in the press.

Inger: Be alert to a possible online scam
From anywhere from Sweden to Saipan,
Asking you to transfer funds of some amount
From a frozen fund to your account.

Virgil: Something needs to be said
About invasion of home and bed

Via beams from gadgets galore,
Seeping through walls, roof, and floor,
So folks don't sit and talk,
Or go for a casual walk
Without gadgets to read or text,
My heavens, what will be next?

Lolo: Folks won't waste time, brother,
Talking to one another.

8

SMOKEY NARRATES ON NATURE'S NORMS

Of a rattlesnake who eats a rabbit,
And a boy who tries to thwart the habit,
Of a Pima tale of how snakes grew fangs
On which our respect for them hangs.
Then, Smokey tells of a hunting pitfall,
Call it a sow's kiss, or a very close call,
Ending with Lupe's ancient Gypsy tale,
Of animals not hesitant to wail
About the Christian, Hindu, and Jew,
As seen from the beast's point-of-view.

All: Open the vents, Roberto!
　　Let some fresh air in,
　　Open the vents, Roberto!
　　Let some fresh air in.

Bob: Okay! Okay! Cut the choral dint,
Okay! Okay! I can take a hint,
You know, narration isn't all glamour,
What with all the choral clamor,
If I'm not careful, I might blow
The intro of our friend with the '*Fro*,
Please hold your horses and shut your face,
So I can do my job with a bit of grace.
Ah-ump! Here's Professor Smokey Cloud,
Who sits in a chair that's been endowed.
Smokey, you tell me if I'm sounding the fool,
I want you to know I think it be cool

To say: you're as Negroid-black as can be,
As ebony-black as Muhammad Alí,
Why, you're the spiting image of Malcolm X,
Over which you never seem to vex,
And, you don't shuck and jive, or do the dozen,
You're not urban-black or even a cousin
To your blood brothers in the inner city,
Don't you think that's a doggone pity?

Smokey: Bob, you don't have
            any black marks with me,
My dark skin is as clear as night to see,
So don't let my ebony color fool you,
Nor my kinky, Afro hairdo.
I'm as much Cherokee as I can be
From a former African slave set free.
I take my Negroid looks from my Gran' Ma,
And, she took her looks from a Cherokee Pa
Who was an African slave from Muskogee,
Owned by a master who was Cherokee.
The Cherokees fought on the Confederate side,
With Abolition they wouldn't abide,
But, once they knew the Civil War was done,
That the Rebs had lost, and the Yanks had won,
They set their slaves free, letting them all go
Without turning their slaves into a foe.
In fact, some Cherokees married their slaves,
Making Africans like me Cherokee Braves.
Some Okies claim to have Cherokee blood,
But it rarely comes from a Cherokee stud.

They claim it comes from a Cherokee princess,
Which, for most, would've been hard to finesse,

Since Cherokees never had a queen or king,
Nobility was a European thing.
What many ordinary Okies know
Is that they have the blood of a Negro,
So a trace of noble blood helps them save face
And gives them prestige in the human race.
Some time ago, an Okie redneck asked me
To show him the next pure Indian I see,
That is, we were just standing there on the walk,
Shoot! I can't recall how we got in a talk.
In a sidewalk crowd, he asked me to point out
At least one pure Indian that was about,
I reversed the question, turned it upright,
And asked if he could point out a pure White.

He gazed at the crowd, and then said, "I cain't,
They ain't got signs on them printed in paint."
I suppose some can claim a thoroughbred line,
Though we've been mixed and mingled a long time,
But then, who am I to call the pot black,
When we're in fact, part of the same pack?
I guess being noble can't be that bad,
I claim to have a Cherokee Great-Granddad.
Speaking of Great-Granddad, *Old Man,* we called him,
He could tell a tale at a wisp of a whim,
At the wink of an eye, at the shake of a hand,
He was up and ready to take the stand,
Though sometimes you had to egg him on
Before he'd fade back into days bygone:
"Old Man, please tell a tale, you're so good,
Before you forget and turn to wood."

Ha! The wooden Indian jab made him mad,
So he'd start a saga and made us glad.

Mother Earth's Gift to Give

I wasn't always an old man, you know?
I was once young, like you, and eager to sow,
To cast my seeds to the wind, to let them blow,
To challenge life that was on the come and go.
Once I felt empty, dry as a skeleton's bone,
Drained and hollow, lonely and alone,
I sought solace in the *Sangre de Cristo* Range
Far from my shanty on the grange,
When I came upon tiny bunnies at play,
Right at the peak of spring in late May.

They were bouncing like balls of rubber,
Blitzing speedily toward each other
As if to collide, smashing, bashing head-on,
Then, they'd jump aside and roll, on-and-on.
Nearby, a rattler watched them at play,
Waiting for a bunny to roll his way,
He appeared to be somewhat sluggish and slow
Compared to the three bunnies on the go.
One bunny bungled. She took a hop
And rolled close to the snake. She couldn't stop.
The rattler slithered toward the bunny,
Peaches and cream, straight for the honey!
The bunny hunkered on the ground, playing dead,
The other bunnies froze. Faces filled with dread,
We heard, "*chi-chi-chi-chi,*" a chilling sound
As the snake circled himself, coiled around
And sprang! Struck! Recoiled,
Striking again, not to be foiled,

The bunny squirmed. Stopped in her stead,
Her body relaxed…limp…she was dead.
The snake sucked the bunny into his throat,

Her legs wiggled. His throat began to bloat,
His tail twitched, the jiggle of a spastic nerve
As his rattles shook, vibrating with verve,
Chi-chi-chi-chi-chi-chi-chi-chi-chi-chi,
The other bunnies stared with startled eyes,
Stunned…stumped…mesmerized,
Chi-chi-chi—They broke his spell and dashed away,
While he gazed-on, each went her way.

Leaving nothing to chance,
I poked about to find a sturdy branch
And returned quickly to the scene of the crime,
Looking for clues. I found a wavy sign,
He was heavy with the bunny
Making his path in the sand easy to see.
Using the stout end of the stiff stick,
I whacked his head, a hard lick!
He rolled and drew-up into a coil,
He was hard to see, blending with the soil,
Whack! He struggled to hold up his head, whack!
Again and again, in swatting attack,
Whack! Whack! I swatted him as he rattled,
He wobbled like a punch drunk embattled,
Rattling a frenetic, frenzied sound,
I'd have to kill him before he gave ground.
He staged an intrepid fight to survive,
Withstanding the whacks, barely alive.

The snake struggled for the right to his space
And did not falter to keep his place,
Whack! Whack! Whack! Whack!
He died. I stopped my attack.
Did I ever feel good! And I knew why,
My adrenaline flowed freely! I was high,

The blood of my ancestors at full flow,
Taking me, the hunter, to a higher glow.
Hey-yeah! It was great to be alive and young,
Though my spring had been thoroughly sprung,
And again I slipped into a morbid zone,
Empty, hollow...alone.

Gnats flew around my face and into my nose,
Making me sneeze and lose repose,
Ahead, heat waves shimmered from the canyon walls
As a herd of sheep made their bleating calls:
Baa ~ baa ~ baa ~ they bleated plodding along,
Butting each other as they bleated their song.
Behind the sheep plodded an ancient man
With a scampi dog that limped as it ran,
Glad to see the shepherd, I started talking,
Saying, "don't worry about where you're walking,
I killed that rattler; I whacked him dead,
His bite is nothing for you to fear or dread."

For a long, long spell the old man was still,
Mulling over my executed kill....

"Paah!" the old man blurted, glancing at the snake,
Asking, "did you kill it for your own sake?"

I was perplexed. I thought he would be glad,
Instead, he was brash yet sad,
As though I had committed a bad act,
When all I'd done was kill a snake, in fact.

"But-but, he ate the bunny," I sputtered,
"Paah! The snake meant no malice," he uttered,

"It was meant to be. He killed to live,
The bunny was Mother Earth's gift to give."

Again, I was confused by the words I heard,
So asked where he was taking his herd.
"Away from this place. Where, I don't know?
I just know the coyotes here make us go."

That's when I noticed the dog had a limp,
Although he was agile for a gimp,
Romping about, keeping the sheep in place,
By nipping their heels, the sheep kept in pace.
Sometimes a sheep would stray and wander away,
Making the sheep a coyote's easy prey.
"What's the matter with your scampy dog?
Did he get caught in a trap or cog?"

"Yes, Solo does have a limp in his scamper,"
The shepherd said sadly, "but it doesn't hamper,
Or stop him from keeping the sheep in line,
Solo is a good sheep dog, a fine canine.
A rancher put coyote bait in a bear trap,
When the bait's tapped, the bear-claws snap.
Solo here, like any dog, went for the bait,
And jammed his paw in the trap before he ate,
When I found him, he'd worked up a lather
By trying to gnaw his paw loose, I gather.

He wouldn't let me sit near the trap,
When I first tried, he'd snarl and snap,
I sat back and waited a long time,
Letting Solo see I'm not the hurting kind.

At last, he let me open the trap
Without so much as a snarl or snap,
His left forepaw was in pretty bad shape,
I picked him up, took him by the nape,
At the time, Solo's paw was a bloody stub,
Quite a price to pay for a little grub.
I took him to the horse doctor in town,
Who looked him over with a wrinkled frown,
Said Solo couldn't make it in the wild
And could put him to sleep with something mild.
Solo's life was not within me to decide,
In Mother Earth, that's where the powers reside,
If Mother Earth meant for Solo to live,
She would decide, it was her gift to give,
And besides, he was still alive, not dead,
So I took him home to nurse, instead,
Not too long before he was up and around,
Ready to herd the sheep that could be found.
Now we must go. We've dallied here too long
Speaking with you, who's got it all wrong.
Don't you know? We're sojourners on this earth,
Fated to wander from the day of our birth,
We must care to live and let live,
Life is a gift for Mother Earth to give."

Then, the old man, Solo and the sheep moved on,
Fading away like a bitter, sweet song.
I wondered how the old shepherd could think
So deeply of what I did in a wink?
I slipped back into that morbid zone,
Drained dry, hollow, lonely, and alone.

Buster: Boy howdy, the young man did interfere
And deserves a sure, swift kick in the rear,

For trying to subdue and suppress,
Attempting to tame the wilderness.

Smokey: Great-Grandpa told me, when I was a child,
The out-of-doors are not untamed wild,
Yet, over this tale I've often wondered,
Why the young man so mightily thundered
Against such an elemental plan
That sets the balance for beast and man.

Lupe: *¿Quién sabe?* The boy was not acting alone,
The ranchers thought nothing of breaking a bone,
They were the ones who were the hip-shooters,
They, not the coyotes, were the intruders.

Inger: We *are* interlopers, for what it's worth,
Destined to wander over the Good Earth,
Even if monuments are made in our name,
And we achieve praise, plaudits, and fame,
These are ephemeral and will soon pass,
Vaporizing into the celestial gas.

Smokey: Humans as interlopers,
A critter that doesn't belong
Where it lopes? That's wrong.
We humans belong on earth
As a part, for what it's worth,
But not "apart" from others
Born of fathers and mothers.
We're just on top the food chain,
Living and dying in sunshine and rain,
And we musn't think we're the best
Among other critters as we nest,

Like all the rest, on Mother Earth,
A place of life, death, and rebirth.

Virgil: Was your tale from Old Man Coyote,
Who'd pull a prank, trip a trap, and gloat?

Smokey: Old Man Coyote
                  was an all-around good guy rogue,
With the Plains Indians, he was more than a vogue,
He was sometimes good, or bad, or in-between,
When big things happened, he was on the scene.
They say when Old Man Coyote was in a squeeze,
He'd spew a wet and windy sneeze,
Causing the wind to bear clouds and warm rain,
Which fell as gully-washers on the plain,
Sometimes he'd cough, causing his nose to blow
And throw a tremendous tornado.
This next tale was cooked up by Great-Granddad,
About what happened when he was a lad,
He based it on a tale the Pimas told
Of rowdy rabbits in the days of old,
Plunking plenty of problems in their wake
By not respecting their brothers the snake.

How Snakes Grew Fangs & Rattles
Long before time was put in a bottle,
Before humans had learned to toddle,
Before war and famine were a concern,
After dinosaurs disappeared from the fern,
After glaciers receded to the North Pole,
Gouging many a moraine, lake, and hole,
After the great Mammoth marauded the land,
And preyed, and was preyed upon, by Folsom Man,

Creatures in the land of quaking aspen,
Creatures in the land of the midnight sun,
Creatures of the sugar maple and oak,
And creatures that lived in the swampy soak,
All were supposed to respect one another,
Sharing the world like sister and brother.
Just as the tide rises and falls each day,
Coming and going without keeping its stay,
Just as the sun and stars always burn bright,
Providing heat in day and light at night,
The rabbits failed the snakes in one aspect
By failing to show them mutual respect,
That is, the rabbits got rough with the snake,
Whose groveling life was no piece of cake.
The slinky snakes ate off the ground
Any meager morsels that were around,
For a home, they had to live in a hole
Just like a common, ordinary mole,
To make things worse, the rabbits would play
By shaking the snakes in flog and flay,
The rabbits got their kicks, it was plain to see,
By whipping each other, with the snakes, into a frenzy.

Now, the snakes didn't have much'a recourse,
Why not? They didn't have fangs, to their remorse,
'Cuz the Great Creator didn't care much for fangs,
Although the snakes were subjected to the pangs
Of bruises and bumps of outrageous play,
By rabbits who used snakes to flog and flay.
Some snakes sought the Creator on their behest,
To give them fangs was their humble request.
Creator caved-in and to fangs said *'okay'*

So long as others were kept from harm's way,
And, He gave them rattles to shake about
As a way to warn others, "*beware to bout,*"
They should shake their rattles, that is to say,
"*Don't crowd me mister, or use me to play.*"

On their intentions, rattlesnakes must tattle,
Before they strike and bite, they must rattle,
Giving the aggressor a second chance
To back away from a battle stance.
The happy rattlesnakes slithered to their holes
Contented to live like ordinary moles,
Slithering to eat as they come and go,
Without worrying about the whipping woe.

The rabbits thought they were really hip,
So, again, they shook the snakes as a whip,
And when the snakes started their tattle-rattle,
The rabbits intensified their prattle,
Whipping each other as hard as can be
Into a fanatical, frenzied glee.
The rest is history. The snakes rattled, then bit,
Putting rabbits into a deadly fit.
Thereafter, rabbits started giving snakes the slip
Without using them to flog, flay, or whip.

Tom: Mercy! The good guy's a snake,
    For some cats, that's tough to take.

Bob: Mixing the gory with the allegory
Makes for one heck of an exciting story,
But is it accurate for me to say,
Allegory's not the Indian way?

Smokey: Yes, you're accurate when you say
Allegory's not the Indian way,
Yet, I had a close call, once, with a bear,
Throwing me into a mighty scare,
Nudging me to ponder about how
There's allegory in the snout of a sow.

Mama Bear Smooches Smokey

The morning of my very first turkey hunt
Was uneventful till I heard a grunt,
Some critter came crashing through the brush,
Breaking the silence of the autumn hush,
At twenty yards away, it came into sight,
Making its way through the brush and light,
A huge three hundred pound mama bear,
Headed on a trail toward my lair
To my cozy, camouflaged nest on the ground,
Where I waited for turkeys to come around.
My 20-gauge shotgun shrank in my hand,
Me sweating like Custer at his Last Stand,
Pondering, *where'n heck did that bear come from,*
Without giving me a chance to hide or run?
At least, there aren't any baby cubs, I thought,
When three cubs showed up! Running at a trot!

They scooted right up to where I sat,
Like so many cats, and I—the rat,
They could play with me all they wanted to,
And there wasn't much I could do.
When a sow and her cubs are close to you,
You have to play it dead without a coup,

Any sudden moves or noises on your part
Could cause the sow to rip-out your heart.
Every nerve in my body was tense and tight
Without the ways and means to take flight,
As I prayed to the Creator for advice,
The mama bear paced around me once…twice,
Her hot, bad breath berating my face,
While she circled around me in precision pace.

Then, she pressed her wet nose to my cheek,
Couldn't remember when things looked so bleak,
This was it—*Great Creator here I come,*
To join my ancestors beyond the sun.
When, all-a-sudden, one cub ran away,
And the other two followed, eager to play,
The sow, too, ambled to gather them up,
Forgetting to claw me for her sup.
Guess I wasn't her kind of manly type
To gorge down her tremendous tripe,
Maybe, she didn't like my black skin or smell?
Paah! Who cares? I was alive and feeling swell.

Tom: Hey! No way, Jose!

Smokey: Yes, way Jose,
The tale's true,
Or my black blood's not blue.

Smokey: Lupe, let's hear that tale from you
Of the Christian, Hindu, and Jew.

Lupe: ¡*Bueno,* hay! I won't say too much,
Just jump into the tale, as such.

Three Tired Travelers

Three tired travelers tramped through a farm
To ask for a room to sleep and keep warm.
"*Sí*," said the farmer, "but before you sleep,
Come in. Sit down. Take a load off your feet,
La Reina has plenty of food to eat,
Tortillas, sopapillas, atolé,
Even a *picoso* pot of *posolé*."
The three tired travelers gladly went in,
Happy to find a cordial host and inn,
The soups zesty, the breads warm,
La Reina cooked with culinary charm.
After they'd supped and made sundry small talk,
The old farmer took them for a short walk,
Out behind the barn, there stood a shanty
No bigger than your grandmother's pantry.
Said the farmer: "two can sleep in the shack,
The other in the barn on a hay rack,
Sorry, the shanty doesn't have more space
Where all of you can sleep in the same place,
So room and board's free, if you wish to stay,
But I won't blame you, if you go away."
The three travelers weren't picky boarders,
Delighted to get free sleeping quarters.

"I'll sleep in the barn," said he who was Hindu,
Leaving the shanty for the other two.

In a lightning flash, the Hindu came back,
Explaining: "I can abide the duck's quack,
Yet to me, cows are sacred. It's taboo
To sleep in their abode, if you're Hindu."
"Don't fret," said the traveler who was Jew,

Leaving the shanty for the other two.
In a short spell, the sleepless Jew came back,
Saying: "I can abide the cattle pack,
Yet, it's not kosher to bed with a hog,
Better to sleep in a hollow log."
"My turn," said the Christian, "as God's my Father,
Neither the cow nor hog is a bother."

Forthwith, the travelers bade their goodnights,
Glad to have resolved their religious plights,
The Christian left to the barn to sleep,
While the others slumbered without a peep.
When the righteous Christian entered the barn,
He muttered a mouthful of muddled yarn:

"Hey! You beasts! Perk up! Be of good cheer!
You can bunk down and sleep without fear,
I'm Christian and love every beast here."
Then with some straw he made a bed to lay,
Knelt down, said his prayers, and hit the hay. . . .
Starry shades of night had barely fallen,
When there arose a boisterous brawling!
"Bang! Bang!" The shanty door was a-shaking,
Awaking the Hindu and Jew, a-quaking.
They opened the door. In stampeded cows,
Goats, hens, ducks, hogs, and some sows!

The squawkings! Mooings! Snorting increased
As the shanty filled with terrified beasts,

Screeching, screaming like a drunken chorus:
"Ack! The Christian! He's liable to eat us!"

Tom: Kudos to the beasts
Cringing from Christian feasts.

Virgil: I'd be willing to bet any fee
That tale was once told by a Gypsy.

Lupe: *O, sí,* the Gypsy is so much a part
Of Spain. Some say it's the heart....

Bob: Lupe halted mid-verse,
Giving new meaning to 'terse.'
Still. The will to tell decreased,
Once again chatter ceased,
Still. Not a burp nor bark,
The van sped through the dark
On a course dimly lit,
The profs content to sit....
After a protracted pause,
Too much telling the cause,
The profs commenced to yell
In a swift, sudden swell.

All: Brrr, Bob, it's cold outside!
Brrr, Bob, close the vents inside!

Bob: Okay! Okay! Ban the banter!
Okay! Okay! Can the canter!
I'll close the vents—halfway,
Still cold? You gotta stay,
Or, move it! Back of the bus,
Don't make a fuss for us.

After closing the air vents about halfway,
And everyone was in place to stay,
We plopped into a prolonged, pensive spell,
Pondering the tale of how rabbits fell.
For a long time everyone was quiet,
Snakes, bears, and bunnies were quite a diet,
As were the caterwauling, cringing beasts
Unwilling to serve the Christian's feast.

9

LOLO POKES FOLKS BIG & SMALL

Of the luscious lyrics of a leery nude,
Who clashes with the rigid teacher Dude,
Preempted by a pope's power grapple
Over belly buttons in the chapel,
Then jokes of a Scotsman, a Lady,
A rotund rogue, and Mrs. Brady.

Bob: Something important we should all know
Of our last storyteller, friend Lolo,
He's a true artist in his own right,
His sketches and drawings are never trite.
He sketched soldiers in the *Death March at Bataan*
In the Pacific Theater with Japan,
He drew the sketches as the men and he marched
Down the Bataan trail, hungry, hot, and parched.
Also, Lolo painted the tragedy at Kent State
That sad day he stood at the entry gate,
Watching as the guardsmen panicked and shot,
Killing four students right there in the lot.
With Lolo his life is also his art,
To him, they can't be split apart.
Lolo, I ask you as an artist, by heck,
Where'd you get the name, '*Lolo Sandec?*'

Lolo: Before my time, Mama went to an op'ra
And fell in love with the name 'Lola.'
I was born a boy, not a girl, so
She managed to call me her little '*Lolo.*'

What "Lola wants, Lola gets," Mama, too,
At least my name isn't 'Sunbonnet Sue.'
I figured, shoot a-mighty, what the heck,
With a moniker like 'Lolo Sandec'

I'd be different from everyone in town,
Flaunting my nimble name like a crown,
Besides, to artists being different is the norm,
Like birds chirping before the raging storm.
By the way, 'Lolo' may be a Nez Perce name,
Upon which I could make a specious claim
To be of the people of the Palouse,
A most fabulous fib! Ah, what's the use?
The first story that I'm going to tell
Is about a brethren artist who fell
Into the cracks when it comes to the arts,
He put the graphics before the charts.

The Nude and the Dude

This one comes from friends at Fredonia-SUNY,
Of a writer who was feeling punk and puny,
He'd written tons of pretty poems and should be glad,
But, no one read them. Egad, too bad, so sad.

He looked for a job that wouldn't tire him out,
Then he could write and generally gad about,
He passed on these jobs listed in the Thrifty Nickel,
Though he knew he was in a dill of a pickle:

"Route driver, Disposal Port-a-Johns, guys or gals,
We provide rigs. You bring nose plugs for smells."

"Summer, Fall fun. Play Keno, work door, floor,
See Perry Pringle, *Publick House*, good benes, more."

"Singer, top dollar, host our Karaoke Nite,
In *Howl @ the Moon Saloon*, can't be uptight."

"Driver, to drive van/profs to conference next week,
All expenses paid, good company, wages bleak."

"Taco Salad Attendant, fix salads and toss,
"*El Cantina Pub, habla español, no mas*."

Then, this ad caught the eye of Peter Pecola,
Like the sound of music from a *Motorola*:

"Teacher Dude Payne wants male model for art class,
To pose nude. Union wages. Can't be lewd or crass."

"It's a cinch," he thought, "this job can't be very tough,
Union wages to sit on my duff in the buff."

Peter P. made a date with Dude Payne, art teacher,
Who was every bit a conservative creature,
"Look here, as the writer, Peter Pecola,
Do you imbibe booze, coffee, or Coca Cola?"

Pete replied demurely, "Never on the job.
Sure, I drink a bit on my own time to hobnob,
Otherwise, on my word, I've a sterile liver,
To my church, I am a regular giver."

Dude Payne replied: "With this job, one can't be too sure,
But, since you give to the church, and otherwise demur

To imbibe in booze, Coca Cola, or caffeine,
The job is yours; you can undress behind the screen.

The class meets in the studio at 10 o'clock,
You might ought-a go home and clean up, somewhat."

Home he dashed to scrub and wash thoroughly
To be bare for budding artists to see!
And thus did Peter Pecola show up,
Eager to undress to make money for his sup.

He undressed, folded his clothes neatly as he could
Standing behind the Chinese screen of silk and wood,
Jumping from behind the screen so as to be seen
He saw a sea of women! He let out a scream!

"Eureka! My papa! No one said to me this class
Would be solitary female students, en masse.
Here I stand before these gals with no clothes on,
This shouldn't happen to a kid from Lake Wobegon,
Dude, this is a bum deal, why didn't you tell me
The only men in this class would be me and thee?"

"Well, Peter you can be safe in a job like this,
Think back to when you were a babe and reminisce,
You were born into the world without clothes and bare,
Yet, your dear mother always gave you tender care,
Washing and cleaning all your private parts that be,
Doing the job, I'm sure, without rancor or glee."

Pete answered immediately,
"Gee, I'm pretty nervous, but I want my fee,
So I'm gonna recite my poetry,

It's pretty good, not too long, and not too quaint,
I'll feel better this way, and the girls can paint
To the cadence of my poem of star-crossed lovers,
In a world of worthless warts and sordid shovers:

Remember where our dreams began?
By that warm, gurgling stream
Who sang to us as she ran,
The songs of the evergreen.
You sang of blues in the night,
I sang of blue moons of lonely days,
We thought of what is—is right
And opposed in many, many ways.
Oh, soon too soon the blizzards came,
Throwing snow and blinding eyes,
Soon too soon hearts were maimed
By soft and mournful cries
of my unforgotten love.

"Stop it! Stop it!" Dude screamed, "before I holler,
I wouldn't give a penny much less a dollar,
To hear such drivel dribble you call poetry,
Affronting pundits progressive in pedantry."

The coeds were vexed by Dude's pretentious pretext,
Creating a coarse, contentious classroom context:
"Why, Professor, with whom have you been schmoozing?
Are you hitting the hooch, bingeing and boozing?

About the verse, we'll be plain, straight and terse,
The nude's bare body compliments his verse.
For an art class on still life, it's been a while
Since we've had a model who's made us smile."

In the classroom, there floated an awkward pause,
A caustic cessation when the mentor's the cause,
Peter P. preempted the silence to butt-in,
Adding percussion to the cacophonous din,
"Hey, Dude, this isn't fair, and you don't really care
To support good literature, no matter how rare."

"Peter P., what you say is nothing but libel,
Why don't you recite poetry from the *Bible?*
At least that way the ladies can proceed to paint,
While quaffing in the words of a prophet or saint."

"Dude, in this class you are the Big Enchilada,
And do decide what's the proper *encantada,*
So it's okay, I'm only in this for the mon,
I'll quote what I know from the *Songs of Solomon*:

How beautiful are your feet in sandals,
O maiden of queenly form!
Your rounded thighs are a jeweled chain,
The work of a master craftsman,
Your navel is as a rounded bowl,
O your belly as a heap of wheat,
Your breasts are as two fawns,
The twins of a gazelle.

"Bravo!" shouted some of the ladies in the class,
"This shrewd nude relates to us like rhythms of jazz,
He can tug at a lady's heart and pull her string,
Doing it with the Bible instead of his thing."

Now Dude felt he was losing control of his class
And needed to quell the ladies
                          without seeming to harass:

"Hmm, let me understand, you think Peter is shrewd,
Because he quotes parts of the *Bible* that are lewd."

"Oh, no! He surely knows other parts as well,
Please give him another chance, for his verse will tell
If he's nothing but a lewd nude on the skids,
Or, a shrewd nude supping with saints,
                                    wearing their bibs."

"Look, rude nude! I'll say it once, and won't enhance,
Because I'm a good guy, I'll give you one more chance,
With the cheeky students—cut the romance!"

"Dude, I don't know where's the hurt, hack, or harm
In quoting Biblical phrases that soothe and charm,
'Cuz these ladies enrolled in Human Drawing 102
Have been around the barn more times than me and you.
Well, shucks, these verses don't speak of women at all,
They're from *Solomon*, of men who are strong and tall:

I adjure you, if you find my lover,
Tell him I am lovesick,
My lover is fair and ruddy,
The choicest among ten thousand,
His head is finest gold,
His locks are wavy, black as ravens,
His eyes are like doves beside brooks of water,
His lips are lilies dropping liquid myrrh,
His body is as polished ivory,
His limbs are pillars of marble—

"Awright! You're fired! Go away! There's just no way
I'll let you spout the verses of men who are gay!

Not in my art class, anyway, I won't have it,
Go on! Get out! Take a trip on a flying ship—"

Before Dude could finish his acerbic harangue,
The indignant ladies jumped in, chanting in chime:
"Boo! Boo! Dude Payne,
You should lower your head in shame,
It's not only the shrewd nude you dare defame,
But a whole class of people who live in our midst,
Because of people like you, their problems persist,
They only want to live and be allowed to love,
Like all of us, they were made by God above."

From the furor, Pecola jumped to his own defense,
Without lugubrious sentiment or pretense:
"Yes, I may be gay, but that's no way
To trash my character and what I say
As perverted. I'm only gay, you know,
And otherwise clean-cut and good, and so
Ashamed to be here in front of these girls,
Threadbare and naked without any frills."

Lolo: I'd like to know from you who are so bright,
Before this trip ends, and we all take flight,
Put your heads together, think with all your might,
How is it that artists fall into such blight?

Lawrence: Should the Dude have shooed the Nude?
And should the Nude have sued the Dude?

Lupe: The shrewd Nude wooed the crude Dude,
The rude Dude shooed the lewd Nude,
Who are we to intrude?

Virgil: Was the Nude lewd or simply shrewd?
Was the Dude crude or simply skewed?

T. Osprey: I wouldn't touch this with a ten foot pole,
Like the guy who fell into his fishing hole,
At first, it seemed simple to him,
But he didn't dog paddle or swim.

Tom: What Dude said about cats who are gay,
I ditto the girls, the Dude should pay.

Buster: We've answered to my satisfaction,
Seems we're getting hard-up for distraction,
Like the rustler wearing the hangman's rope,
We're getting desperate as we lose hope.

Inger: But, that's the way it is with a soap,
There'll always be another ship of hope
To take you through the next titanic trip
That goes on-and-on with unending conflict.

Lolo: There's one virtue an artist can't balk,
He must be willing to walk his talk,
A meal of mush dished by a phony
Is still baloney.
I wouldn't say Nude was overly lewd,
But the Dude was overly rude,
And that's the story's twist,
Dude can't call himself an artist.

All: Well, I suppose,
The guy with the clothes....

Lolo: How did I guess, with my query,

you wouldn't lid
And hammer it down tight? Think I'll tell Uncle Sid.

Uncle Sid's Soap

Uncle Sid was hooked on TV, mostly the soaps,
And also gossiped about petty, pious folks,
More directly, they were post-Renaissance popes
Who patronized a few artists, poets, and goats
And lived in castles circled by holy water moats.
When the ceiling was painted in the Sistine Chapel,
Michelangelo caused a pope's pious grapple,
Depicting the acquisition of Adam's soul
As coming directly from God, making Adam whole.
God is painted floating in a white, velvet cloud,
With some male and female cherubs in the crowd,
Adam is shown nude, protruding from God's finger,
Revealing a belly button and a dinger.
Adam's dutiful dinger didn't disturb the popes,
But, his belly button became the stuff of soaps.

One pope said because "man was made in His image,
Adam's belly button does not fit the visage,
For Adam was not born of woman and should not
Be portrayed as having an umbilical knot.
I will paint over the knot," the pope decreed,
"To enact my belief on the knotty recede."
Another pope decreed: "With belly buttons and art,
They imitate life and shouldn't be taken apart.
Therefore, the navel of Adam will be scraped clean
So his belly button can be clearly seen,
Despite the fact that it will glimmer and gleam."

Of the fresco, we shouldn't speak of theology,
After all, Michelangelo copied his anatomy."

With each new pope there came an old debate,
To paint over Adam's belly button, or scrape?
The next time you go to the Sistine Chapel,
Behold Michelangelo's fresco and grapple
With the important questions and issues of popes,
See how the navel shines! Washed with many soaps.

Bob: Tho' you claim to speak of artists and soaps, You
really took a jab at saintly popes.

Virgil: I don't think Lolo's tale
                          of the pope's pious grapple,
Will do much to illuminate the Sistine Chapel.

Lolo: That was my last story about artists, by heck,
We all know they never play cards with a full deck,
So now, I'll tell you folks about a Scottish rite,
Of what happens when you build a brick wall right.

Mac Croskey's Extra Brick
While there is some truth in a stereotype,
We shouldn't believe all of its hype,
You've heard of the bricklayer's Scottish rite
Of being neat, cheap, frugal, and tight?
Well, when Mac Croskey the Scotsman built a wall,
He wanted it to stand five feet tall,
They say his eyeball was calibrated,
To inform him as he calculated
The exact number of bricks he should buy
To build the wall exactly five feet high.

The bricks delivered, he starts to build,
Deducing how much mortar to yield,

He's proud of the fact he could nit-pick
Without wasting a single ounce of it.
To mix too much mortar is shameful waste
That often happens when you mix in haste.
Before long, the wall's built and starts to cure,
And he's proud of a job well done, to be sure,
Yet, he finds he has one brick in surplus,
Does that mean the brick is worthless?

Knowing about the Scottish stereotype,
About the Scots' penchant to be tight,
Take a wild guess, hurry, and be quick,
What did Mac Croskey do with the extra brick?

Buster: Beings he's so downright tight,
He'd sure as shoot, sell it outright.

T. Osprey: He'd trade it for some fish,
　　　Raw, flayed, or in a dish.

Lolo: You don't get it! You're both wrong, that's okay,
With the extra brick? Why, he'd throw it away.

All: Throw the brick away?
What? Huh? Duh! No way!

Bob: Lolo, boy do I ever have bad news,
I heard the exact same joke about Jews,
About being cheap and making money,
None of us thought it was funny.

Lolo: That's what's wrong with a stereotype,
Especially when you believe all its hype.
Well, so what? The joke didn't pan out,
So I'm blazing a different route,

This next tale's about Mrs. Betsy Brady
And her Chihuahua pooch named '*Lady.*'

Mrs. Brady & Lady the Pooch
To insure Lady didn't lose her spark
Betsy Brady took Lady to the park,
Where they walked among the trees and grass
So Lady could squat down to make her pass.
Owners are supposed to take home the poop,
Which Mrs. Brady did with a doggie scoop.
She and Lady rode the bus to the park,
Daily they boarded at ten o'clock sharp,
Betsy sat next to an open window
With Lady in her lap in the fourth row.

One day as they were riding, oh, so calm,
Looking forward to their walk on the lawn,
A rather rotund man sat next to them
With a lapel stained by a leaky pen.
Otherwise, he was dressed dandy, fit to kill,
From a felt fedora to loafers of eel,
And, he held a lighted cigar in hand,
Huffing and puffing it to beat the band.

Brady's Lady started to hack, cough, and gag,
And her sanguine spirits started to sag.
When Betsy Brady politely asked the man

To dowse the cigar as soon as he can,
He scoffed aloft and blew more smoke,
Causing Lady to sneeze, wheeze and choke.
Then, when he lay the cigar on the ash tray,
Mrs. Betsy Brady thought quickly to say:

"Who's that person outside the window?
Why, I'll be? It's that famous so-and-so,
Jeepers! It's that hubba-hubba singing star,
Ms. Whochee Coochee getting out'a her car."

As the man turned to see the so-and-so,
Betsy threw his cigar outside the window.
The man knew precisely what had occurred,
Why it was that Betsy fibbed and perjured,
For no one famous was out-and-about,
So he in turn thought quickly to shout out:

"Who's that person outside the window?
Why, I'll be? It's that famous so-and-so,

Jeepers! Creepers! The savvy singing stars
Bubba Bromide and gorgeous Gaga Gars. "
Betsy jerked her head around to see,
Falling for the stunt, to the fat man's glee,
As she wiggled to see and look about,
The fat man grabbed Lady and threw her out!

All: Gasp! Egad!
Oh, no! Too bad!

Lolo: "My Lady! My Lady Chihuahua dog
Was thrown out the window by this fat hog!

Stop the bus! Stop the bus! Stop it right here,
Let me off to rescue my little dear."
The bus driver promptly stopped the bus,
His day was long; he didn't need the fuss.
Betsy found Lady at the end of the block,
Chipper and hale and ready to walk.

All: Oh, good!
Glad she could!

Lolo: To Brady's astonishment and surprise,
Lady clenched something in her mouth as a prize,
Try to guess what Lady had in her mouth,
An object well known in the North and South.

Lawrence: Since neither
               could've been thrown too far,
    It must have been the fat man's cigar.

Lolo: Hah! You fell for my trick,
Of course, it was the brick
From the last joke I told,
Dog mouthing brick—behold.

Tom: Zounds! That's classy pool,
     Hep, cool, and drool.

Virgil: I never cared much for fat man jokes,
     Since I are one of those big blokes.

Bob: Lolo, done, huh? Your tales hit the spot Pricking
with *picante*, picky hot
With plenty of levity. They were swell,

Now does anyone have more tales to tell?....
Since there are none, then I have a request,
Let's turn our attention to the contest.
We decided some kind of prize would go
To the best performance telling tales or no.
It's customary to take a straw vote
To see if any teller hit a high note,

We may find one teller to stand out so well,
We needn't wait for the count of the bell.

Virgil: Lawrence weighed in mean
                    and lean, right on scale,
For precision of language and vivid detail.

Lupe: Virgil's imagery and philosophic undertones
Penetrated my soul and permeated my bones.

Lawrence: To me, Inger was the most like Chaucer,
When you look at her whole cup and saucer.

Inger: Here's to T. Osprey for his wacky whimsy,
Though he may mix metaphors and mimsy.

Smokey: Lolo's the winner,
                    for he told the best whoppers,
Of folks with the sense of grasshoppers.

T. Osprey: To Buster, without a doubt,
He should catch the biggest trout.

Buster: My vote goes to our singer,
Sure, Tommy's a humdinger,

But he did compose and sing
As soothing as a starling.

Tom: Though he laid a levy
On our cherry bevy,
I'd give Lupe "A"
For what he had to say.

Lolo: I liked Smokey's rabbit and snake tales,
To him should go the hardiest hales.

Bob: A punctilious, pungent pause pursued,
And I didn't want to appear too rude,
But clearly, the professors couldn't decide
Who chit-chatted the best tale of our ride,
So instead I said:
Hmmm, I can tell you can't agree,
So that leaves the decision up to me.

All: You know, they say when the going gets tough,
The tough get going, and that's good enough.

Bob: Polish polka, Spanish fandango,
        It takes two to tango.

All: Cut the cheese and curds!
Pull the plug on puffy words!

Bob: I'll be screwed and tattooed!
I'll be bellowed and booed!

All: Better cut to the chase,
Tell us who won the race.

Bob: As there is nothing new under the sun,
I declare and declaim: all of you won!

All: Way to go! *Dos-à-dos,*
Roly-poly. Holy-moly,
Scrambled eggs for breakfast.

EPILOGUE

The storytelling contest is done,
The profs could care less who won,
They drift into a restless sleep,
For Bob, demons commence to creep.

We were done. The last story had been told,
We had driven through the night and the cold,
Listening, telling nearly the whole trip,
Rapt in tales, songs, and poems without slip.
One-by-one, the profs drifted into sleep,
A skittish slumber, not very deep,
Just like so many sardines in a can,
Primly packed into the seats of the van,
Dozing in-and-out the edge of wakefulness,
Leaning on each other in tight compress....
Midnight. A bronze moon beamed at full blaze
In a clear dark sky without cloud or haze,
The van rode with hardly a list,
While we cruised amidst a surreal mist
Along fallow fields stubbled in old crops
And sundry stations, cafes, and truck stops.

As the profs dozed, slumping in their seats,
Inger and I felt a need for some treats.
We pulled over to *Reno's Arcade*,
Where Inger and I watched a poignant parade,
Truckers who'd stopped to diesel-up and rest,
The homemade pies, says Reno, were the best:

Rhubarb, mince, banana cream, and cherry,
Apple, peach, pecan, and boysenberry.
Some truckers sat at tables, talking roads,
Weather conditions, patrolmen, and cargo loads,
Some had stopped to change clothes and shower,
Drink coffee and while away the hour.
Some played electronic poker and keno,
On unrigged machines, according to Reno.
On the jukebox, we heard in naïve metaphor:
"Don't come a'knockin' on my front door,
My heart's nuthin' but an empty floor."
All sorts of goodies were displayed for sale,
Razors, toothpaste, and pills for when you ail,
Boots, bandanas, buckles, and hunting knives,
Blouses and lingerie for women and wives.

While we sat, sipped coffee, and munched on pie,
Inger paused and gazed at me, seeming to sigh,
Then said, "before graduate school days
I drove a truck, and remember these stays,
Driving the open road was a lonesome place,
Truck Stops like these were hard to replace,
It got to the point you could hardly wait
For these stops, after driving 8-hours straight."
Just then, a fly dropped from the arcade sky,
Plunging in a spiral, seeming to ply,
Aiming for a crumb on the table top,
"A sight you'd see," Inger said, "at any stop,
Birthing, dying, they live here year round,
Eating bits of crumbs and crust that abound."

Something there was about this transient stay
That hastened us on our solitary way,

The truckers were oblivious to us there,
Recreating a bit in the smoky air,
Listening and talking in subdued tones,
Slightly louder than the truckers on phones:
"If you're goin' south, there's a speed trap ahead,
Got it from Delbert doing deadhead.
You gotta go the speeds the signs tell you,
If 'n you don't, you're a fool, or a durned old mule."
During our brief stay, it didn't seem odd
That Inger once handled a trucker's job,
This late at night, somehow, she was in place,
Taking a pause to muse the trucker's pace.
Outside, the trucks idled, loaded with goods,
Destined to serve sundry neighborhoods.
The deep rattle of their engines at idle
Pinged in a jangling, clanging recital,
Time it was for us to be on our way
To head south to the city by the bay.

Back on the road again, Inger dozed off,
At times, she would mumble, moan, or cough.
Three a.m. We drove around Sacramento,
Noticed the gasoline gauge was dropping low,
Filled up the tank. It didn't take too long
To get back on I-80. I hungered for song,
Jiggled the A.M./F.M. radio dial
Looking to listen to music a while,
Picked up a talk show from Mexicali
About bacteria in the belly,
It seems there's an antibiotic cure
For ulcers—kills the germ bugs, as it were.
Another station played moody, velour tunes,
Recordings resembling the croons of loons.

Tired of the tunes. Turned the radio off,
In the quiet I heard a sigh, a cough,
In silence driving into dawn, I could feel
A demise—the passing of the surreal.
We approached a steep hill and dropped to low gear,
Climbing the grade, the van strained, we were near,
There, in the early morning fog, she lay,
Half awake…asleep…the city by the bay.
Spaniards set her up in 1776,
Long before the 49'ers and their picks,
Burned down by fire in 1906,
Right after big earthquakes put in their licks.
After the quakes, she was rebuilt from scratch,
Like the town of old, with a spirit to match,
People here are known for their diversities,
Financial centers, and universities,
Old timers say, there are days it hasn't rained,
Fog's gone, sun's out, it's paradise regained.

Wasn't long we were cruising through the suburbs,
With their manicured lawns and rounded curbs,
Each of the profs was slowly awaking,
Muttering, as they were making, shaping
A schedule of how each would spend the day,
Determined to make the best of this stay.

T. Osprey: Later today, I'll make a presentation,
    A summary of my dissertation.

Lupe: I'm going onto the UC campus,
To visit some old colleagues that I miss
From way back when, Chicano Protest Days,
We drew from the campus in many ways.

Buster: Think I'll join you to go over to UC,
   To see friends in animal physiology.

Lolo: I'll be down in the Silicon Valley,
Looking for graphic ware, anyone join me?

Virgil: I'll go with you Lolo,
I need to find some interactive video
To use on my Latin TV show.

Lawrence: I'll be at a daylong session on the Internet,
With cyber-crimes,
              we haven't scratched the surface, yet.

Tom: I'm with Larry and the cyber-crime thing,
There's a growing group, a technocratic ring
Of keyboard hackers and money backers,
Trying to steal what we know
By ripping off the information flow.

Smokey: I'm interested in the Internet, too,
Mainly, though, as a story-sharing tool.

Inger: Hope you don't mind if I join you boys?
I recently bought me one of those toys,
You know? A handy laptop computer,
And I'll want your help to boot her.

Lolo: Say Bob, grab a laptop, write up this trip
Of our tales and quips full of hip and zip,
Don't just copy our phrases and lines,
Fix up the mangled meters and rhyme crimes.

Tom: Hey, yeah, man, write of the jammin' good time
We've had telling tales in rhythm and rhyme.

Bob: I decided to ignore their remarks,
To keep alert for signs and landmarks,
Thus far, I'd done well as pilot of this ship
And wanted to end the trip without a blip.
Anyway, they might not like the gabble
I write about their penchant to babble,
Though it sounded like serious fun
To write about telling tales on the run.
Of course, I'd be lucky if anyone
Under the sun would even read one
Maudlin tale before becoming undone,
Throwing the book in a garbage heap—
I'd have to publish it on the cheap.

I pulled off Powell to the *Mark Hopkins,*
Struggled with bags through the door that spins,
Into the lobby, we approached the desk,
Rooms had been reserved at Lupe's request.
The rent for my room was split by the men,
Inger complimented my narrative yen,
Then, each of the professors went their way,
Agreeing to meet at the close of day.
At the door to my room, I swiped the plastic card,
A green light blinked, I pushed softly, then hard,
Yet the door didn't budge. I swiped again, *Nada.*
Third time's a charm. Swiped again
And the door opened to the cavernous room,
King size beds, love seat sofa, and shiny bathroom,
A wraparound corner computer station,
Huge flat screen flashing an equation,

<VC=VT> and the message "strike any key to seize
Virtual Conference Equals Vital Technologies."
Dropped my bag and sat at the monitor,
Punched the "K" key, listening to the whir
Of the computer boot-up its message:
"You need not be a geek, guru, or sage,"
Text and speech simultaneous from the screen,
"At the computer desk you'll be seen,
And, you'll see and hear other conferees
Who've downloaded papers and paid their fees.
This is teleconferencing at its premier,
In fact, you might be anywhere but here
If you had Vital Technologies at hand
To confer wherever you sit or stand.

Presenters: using the Kwik-Pic scanner,
Enter your paper with its rubric banner
Into the Virtual Conference data base,
Where you'll be able to encode your case.
If you want to read along as you scan,
Or make prefatory remarks, you can
If you remain before the monitor
Where others may stay as you confer."
Yuk! I shoved away from the monitor,
Cold and clammy, no amount of fur
Could coat the scathing chill of cyber space
While the monitor faded to its pallid, drab face.
Just then my cell phone hummed,
I answered fast. I was bummed
To hear a computerized voice
Asking me to make some choice,
What I needed more than anything
Was to press the flesh, to laugh and sing.

Flushing the toilet with superfluous zeal
I wondered *what in this sterile room is real?*
The plumbing seemed real. I took a shower,
Shaved, and daubed cologne smelling of flower,
Don't ask which kind, rose, dahlia, or daisy,
By now I was feeling a bit hazy,
Naked and hollow, I was stripped bare
In many more ways I dare or care
To say even though I was fully dressed,
And inured, I thought, by our story fest
Of a room bereft of human contact
Among machines to relate and interact,
No wonder the profs planned to go places,
Visit old haunts, old friends, and meet new faces.

Ducked out the room. Rode the elevator
To the lobby where I spied a waiter,
Towering and handsome, brown curly hair,
White shirt and vest, black slacks pressed with care,
He deftly described an easy way
For me to make a breakfast getaway.
Outside the hotel, sparrows chirped wildly,
The fog was lifting; a breeze blew mildly,
I hopped on a cable car to North Beach
Where breakfast prices were within my reach.
Sitting there, I nodded in-and-out of sleep,
The caffeine's power had begun to creep,
To slip away, and again I could feel
A loss—the gradual demise of the surreal—
As I slumped and dozed in the cozy cable car
Hoping North Beach wasn't too far.
Got off for a café, decided to go
Toward the smell of fresh baking bread dough.

As I walked along, these scenes exploded,
Stabbing my eyes, my aura imploded:

An unkept man slept in a basement nook,
I guess he slept. I didn't care to look,
Or to check his pulse in the enclosure,
Perhaps he'd died from hunger or exposure.

A woman in combat fatigues and boots,
Pilfered through a garbage can with her troops,
A small boy and girl in denim jackets,
Culling lettuce from disposed food packets.

A Guatemalan group sang to sell CDs and tapes,
Describing decapitations and rapes
By right wing government agents who led
A campaign against those peasants who read.

A Mom & Pop store was papered with signs,
Posters offering rewards of all kinds,
For young boys and girls of every race,
Who'd disappeared, abducted without trace.

I shrugged to shake these sad scenes from my head,
They boomeranged and circled back instead,
Much like a lighted bus passing at night,
Where we see folks fleeting from our sight
On their discrete missions down the dark street,
Each with a story to recall or repeat,
And only for a brief moment do we see
One passing episode of their entirety
Before they slip from beneath the light
Into the murky shadows of the night.

Made in the USA
Charleston, SC
20 November 2016